Huma

Divine Redemption

The Theology and Practice of the Examen

By Marko Ivan Rupnik, SJ

With a Foreword by James Martin, SJ

Pauline
BOOKS & MEDIA

Library of Congress Cataloging-in-Publication Data

Rupnik, Marko Ivan, 1954-
  [Esame di coscienza. English]
    Human frailty, divine redemption : the theology and practice of the examen / Marko
Ivan Rupnik ; with a foreword by James Martin. ~ 1st English ed.
    p. cm.
  ISBN 0-8198-3410-6 (pbk.)
  1. Conscience, Examination of. I. Title.
BX2377.R8713 2011
264'.020861~dc23

                                    2011018057

The Scripture quotations contained herein are from the *New Revised Standard Version
Bible: Catholic Edition*, copyright © 1989, 1993, Division of Christian Education of the
National Council of the Churches of Christ in the United States of America. Used by
permission. All rights reserved.

Excerpts from the English translation of the *Catechism of the Catholic Church* for use in
the United States of America, copyright © 1994, United States Catholic Conference,
Inc.—Libreria Editrice Vaticana. Used with permission.

Cover design by Rosana Usselmann

Cover: Detail of mosaic by Marko Ivan Rupnick, SJ,
          Atelier del Centro Aletti. Photo by Aurelio Amendola.

"P" and PAULINE are registered trademarks of the Daughters of St. Paul.

Translated by Matthew Sherry

Original edition title: *L'esame di Coscienza, per vivere da redenti* by M. I. Rupnik

Copyright © Lipa srl, Published by Lipa srl, 25 Paolina

First English edition, 2011

Published by Pauline Books & Media, 50 Saint Pauls Avenue, Boston, MA 02130-3491
Printed in the U.S.A.

www.pauline.org

Pauline Books & Media is the publishing house of the Daughters of St. Paul, an
international congregation of women religious serving the Church with the
communications media.

1 2 3 4 5 6 7 8 9   15 14 13 12 11

Contents

PART ONE

THE EXAMINATION OF CONSCIENCE: THEOLOGICAL FOUNDATIONS

PART TWO

THE SPIRITUAL LIFE
AND THE EXAMINATION OF CONSCIENCE

PART THREE

MAKING THE EXAMINATION

Foreword

Too many Christians think they don't pray well. Or that they are praying "wrong." Or that everyone else probably has an easier time praying.

That's why Father Marko Rupnik's new book is a godsend—almost literally. For it will introduce you to a kind of prayer that anyone can do. Whether you've been on many retreats, or are just beginning to include prayer in your daily life, the examen is a wonderful—and easy—support for your spiritual life.

Although Catholics had been using this kind of prayer for centuries, it came to be associated with St. Ignatius of Loyola, the sixteenth-century founder of the Jesuit Order, who popularized it. In addition to the Mass, Saint Ignatius used to say that the examen is the one prayer that a Jesuit should never omit from his day.

The examen is a prayer that enables us to see where God has *been*. And this is usually far easier than recognizing God in the present, since we're typically so distracted and preoccupied by our daily tasks.

In the Book of Exodus, for example, God says to Moses, "You cannot see my face." How often that is the case with us! We may feel unable to see God as the day's events are unfolding. But that same God then allows Moses to see him pass. This "passage" is a gentle reminder that it is sometimes easier to see God in retrospect than in the moment.

Father Rupnik, a brother Jesuit, has long been one of my favorite Christian artists. I have marveled at his astonishingly beautiful mosaics both on the façade of the Basilica of the Holy Rosary in Lourdes and in the Chapel of the Holy Spirit at Sacred Heart University in Connecticut. His bold portrayals of Jesus, the Blessed Mother, and the saints speak directly to my heart. He is a gifted artist.

My Jesuit brother is also a gifted spiritual guide, and his new book will help you not only do "the basics," but go deeper. He will help you see the examen as a way to discern, that is, to make life-giving decisions and see more clearly God's desires for you. He will help you understand it as a step on the way to the redemption that Christ won for us. And he will help you appreciate it as a way of entering more deeply into the mystery of the "Body of Christ," which is the Church.

Most of all, this beautiful new book will help you draw closer to God.

JAMES MARTIN, SJ

James Martin, SJ is a Jesuit priest and author of numerous books on spirituality, including The Jesuit Guide to (Almost) Everything *and* My Life with the Saints

Introduction

In a well-known article published in 1972, Father George Aschenbrenner noted a general crisis, widespread in the Church, in the practice of the examination of conscience.[1] To a great extent the exaggerated sense of moralism and legalism that once accompanied this exercise—and its almost exclusive use within the context of confession—brought about this crisis. Practiced in this way, the examination of conscience sometimes produced such side effects as scrupulosity, depression, and discouragement—in some cases approaching pathological anxiety. Then the pendulum swung the other way. A spirituality mainly rooted in morality and willpower was swept away by a rediscovery of psychology, which practically replaced the spiritual life and presented itself as a kind of secularized spirituality. The practice of the examination of conscience was then caught up in the same wave of reaction and replaced by psychological exercises of self-observation and "mental hygiene." But now this fad is also dying out. So pastors of souls, formation directors, and, above all, the faithful feel the need to rediscover ways, means, and instruments to further these ends: to foster spiritual maturity, to sustain their journey of spiritual growth in order to live as redeemed persons in the modern world, and to bring to fruition the vocation entrusted by God to each person for the good of the Church and humanity. And so the subject of the examination of conscience is resurfacing. Previous generations detached the examen from an organic vision of the spiritual life and from its theological-anthropological framework. But that does not mean we can close the door on this spiritual practice, which has existed since the beginning of the Christian faith and been practiced by the great masters of the spiritual life.

Just as a precious gem shines in all its splendor when properly set, I have dedicated a major portion of this book to the theological and spiritual context in which the examination of conscience should be placed. Even though we may be tempted to try to learn immediately how to carry out this exercise, I invite the reader to spend time on the first part of the book. The examination of conscience is best understood and practiced correctly when it is an organic part of the vision revealed through theological foundations.

By reading the text as presented,[2] the reader will be able to approach the examen as a spiritual art of prayer and discernment, which deepens each person's journey of redemption. The reader will understand the natural connection of this exercise to the entire body of the Church. He or she will experience the grace of a journey in virtue, purification from evil, and constant progress toward conformity to the image of the triune God, which renders us capable of living his image within the community.

Like the Church, the human community suffers greatly from the complex problems of today's world. If we realize the urgent need to begin working on ourselves—including our need for a new sensitivity to moral questions—it is necessary to propose authentic spiritual paths to follow and thus avoid new forms of moralism.

PART ONE

The Examination of Conscience: Theological Foundations

Memory and the Examination of Conscience

The woman who lost her coin and began to search for it with a lamp would never have found it if she had not remembered it. And when she had found it, how could she have known whether it was hers if she had not remembered it? I remember having lost many things and having looked for and found them; and I know that when I was searching for any of them and was asked: "Is this it? Is that it?" I answered, "No," until what I was searching for was presented to me. But if I had not remembered it—whatever it was—I would not have found it, because I could not have recognized it, even if it had been shown to me. And this is the way it always is when one loses something, searches for it, and finds it.

If anything, for example, a visible object, disappears from our view, but not from our memory, its image is preserved within us, and so we look for it until we see it again. And when we find it, we recognize it thanks to the image we carry inside ourselves; we could not say that we have found the object if we do not recognize it. It was, in fact, gone from our sight, but still present in our memory. [3]

Augustine

Saint Augustine emphasizes the indispensable role of memory in the process of knowledge. Memory is based on experience. It is the dimension of our intellect that grounds awareness in experience. Through experience, our memory constantly connects our mind to life; it keeps our reflection, speculation, and reasoning attached to life. Life is communicated through interpersonal relationships—even a child's birth depends on the communication between two persons, on their relationship. A person's life is founded on the relationships he or she establishes with other people, creation, self, and God. We live because the Creator enters into relationship with us, his creatures. This relationship is the living source that seals the mystery of life with love and the ability to relate and communicate.

However, since relationships are exposed to sin and evil, it follows that the human memory cannot escape this fate. Once the memory has been disturbed or wounded, we cannot simply correct it by means of reasoning or self-understanding, as if we had the ability to determine its content.

Since the memory is directly connected to life, it seems to act on two levels. On the one hand, it is a completely human activity, because it originates from our intellect and is based on our experience. On the other hand, it is open to that boundless mystery to which life itself introduces us, because life constantly leads us to a threshold, a boundary from which it stretches out to us: life comes, visits, and is given to us; in a certain sense we possess and direct life, but our experience forces us to admit it is impossible to exercise dominion over it. And what we can't dominate in life, what leads us to intuit this openness, is precisely the mystery of free relationships, of love—that is, of the other. Ultimately it is the mystery of God, the Lord of life.

As Saint Augustine says shortly after the passage quoted earlier, we cannot find God directly within our memory. But just as we are certain that God gives us life, calls us into existence, creates us in his image, and redeems us, we are certain that God communicates himself to us. So, in a way, we can say that God lives in our memory—just as all of sacred Scripture is the memory of God's action in human history. In fact, religion is largely a memory of God's activity. God's communication, this grace given to us by God who is moved by love for his creatures, and this welcoming of his communication, of his gift, the memory of this divine-human relationship, is precisely the Wisdom of God. Under one aspect, this pertains entirely to God, and under another it grows and expands throughout human history as a divine gift that we can consciously grasp, treasuring it in our hearts as an understanding of faith and agape.

Maturing as God's Image

> Created in God's image, the human person matures by using this divine image as a point of reference. "We say, in fact, that God and man serve as each other's model, and that God humanizes himself for man, in his love for man, to the same extent to which man, strengthened by charity and with God's help, divinizes himself."[4]
>
> *Maximus the Confessor*

The human person grows in a complete and integral way in reference to this eternal Wisdom, recognizing both what fosters true life and what is illusory, deceptive, and idolatrous. It is natural for a human being to seek a point of reference. Created in the image of God, the human person should not do less than compare him or herself to the Prototype, the Original of whom he or she is the image. By nature, we constantly tend to look up to a model. Now, if this point of reference is Christ, the Son of God, in whom we are created, that is one thing. But if we take as our model an illusory, imaginary reality, that is another. If we, the image of God, direct ourselves, our intellect, our gaze, our spirit toward Christ, then we experience our personal history as a story of God's love, which in every instant can transform us. Thus, there is a reciprocity, a dialogue in which we are never alone. Whatever happens to us, whatever sin we might commit, we find ourselves faced with Christ's still more extraordinary action

If we . . . direct ourselves . . . toward Christ, then we experience our personal history as a story of God's love, which in every instant can transform us.

as our Redeemer. We experience the original, to whom we relate as a model—and therefore also as a law—but inseparably united to the merciful Face of Christ, to the perennial gateway to the mercy of God.

Actually, one cannot speak of a model per se when referring to a living and loving Person, an absolutely dynamic reality who is free from any rigidity, any fixed and static notions that would turn us into objects. Given that the Prototype is a living being, the supreme Person in the theological sense, it is evident that we, too—created in God's image—are not static realities that can be analyzed solely on the basis of externals. The image is not a formal imprint, a pattern. It, too, is a living being, a person created as a participant in the same Love that constitutes the divine life. Therefore, the image is a personal being in communion with its Prototype. It is the manifestation of the Prototype, of his creative and redemptive action. Thus, the image possesses the dynamism of an ever increasing assimilation to the Prototype. And this means that the image is fully realized only when it manifests the Prototype.

Instead, we might take as our point of reference an abstract model, such as a code of law or vague, mysterious divinities exposed to impersonal and cosmic powers. But then we will always waver between a legalistic servitude experienced as a sort of straightjacket, and a self-indulgence aimed at giving free reign to our passions and desire for self-assertion. Then we experience either presumption and pride when we manage to live up to the model, or complete depression, a sort of damnation in the face of an implacable universal law, whenever we fail to live up to it. So we either invent compromises to justify our condition, or we accept life as a battlefield of impersonal struggles between good and evil. The image reflects the prototype. If we create our own ideal, we understand ourselves in relation to that. Therefore, if the prototype is an abstract reality, we will regard ourselves in abstract terms. If the prototype is conceived as a formal ideal, we will try to shape ourselves according to that ideal. By this process we imprison or enslave ourselves. This is true even if we decide to live without any point of reference, departing from any ideal or value. For, as images, we always live in relation to whatever reality we have made our dialogue partner in daily life. Those who fashion idols for themselves gradually become like what they have made (see Ps 115:4-8). And Scripture warns that we create idols to gain some benefit from them (see Isa 44:10).

This tendency to create reference points that fundamentally express our own egoism is due to the influence of the tempter. The Fathers of the Church did not hesitate to speak of the fallen angel, the devil, the enemy of human nature. In fact, in our context, the fall of the angels enlightens us. The angels are created as messengers between God and human beings, and, by their nature, they are oriented to their Creator, whom they serve for the good of human beings. In Satan's refusal to serve, he rebels against God and is no longer God's messenger. Satan brings no blessings. But because he, too, was created for relationship, he proposes himself to human beings as a model of self-realization, the epicenter of all things, free from every form of servitude and puffed up with pride. Satan becomes a model of casting off God, of alienation from God, of movement toward self rather than God. The temptation to take as a reference point anyone or anything that is not the living, triune God is always illusory. It's an illusion of relationship, self-offering, and self-sacrifice that eventually shows itself as a dark, devastating force of rebellious egoism.

Let us now explore how, from a theological perspective, it is possible for us to examine our thoughts, emotions, daily activities, and decisions by using an exercise of the memory as described by Saint Augustine. In this way, we will readily see that self-examination is not an isolated act of our reason regarding models of behavior, thought, or action that have been imposed on us or learned in theory. It will become clear that the examen is a prayer, an act that takes place within a strong relationship where the experience of love, redemption, and the truth of life launch us into a process of deepening and developing an always fuller understanding. The examination of conscience is a true encounter with God in Jesus. It enables us to see ourselves in his presence, united with him and with others. Then we will realize that self-

examination within the recesses of the heart also has a social
and ecclesial dimension.

The Other and Others:
A Condition for Self-knowledge

> Love is a real knowledge of the other because this knowl-
> edge coincides with absolute faith in the reality of the
> beloved. In the most general sense, this faith is a rising
> above oneself and a self-renunciation, a reality present in
> the pathos of love itself. The sign of this compenetration is
> found in the absolute affirmation, with one's entire will
> and understanding, of the "you are" of the other's being.
> By uttering this complete affirmation of the other's being—
> in the fullness of which and through which the entire
> content of my own being is stripped away and emptied—
> the other ceases to be foreign to me, and the "you" has
> become for me another description of my "I." "You are"
> means not only "you are acknowledged by me as truly exist-
> ing," but "your being is experienced by me as my own, and
> in your being I understand myself more fully." You are;
> therefore, I am.[5]

> *Vj. I. Ivanov*

Experience, memory, relationship, and understanding
are all intrinsically connected with humans as created persons. Man and woman are knowable through their
relationships with others. Saint Augustine himself says: "You
are; therefore, I am." The person does not know her or himself simply as reflected in a mirror. Rather, a person discovers
his or her true features when face to face with others. Pavel

Florenskij[6] states that knowledge of things differs from knowledge of persons. He emphasizes that the indispensable starting point to knowing others is love.

But it is also true that even to know objects, we need a religious point of departure that recognizes and affirms their independent existence. Only if we have such a relationship with objects can their true inner reality be disclosed to us—a reality in which is hidden the meaning of all existence. Small children talk to everything they encounter. They converse with trees, animals, the snow, the sun, etc. In a certain sense, genuine Gospel wisdom does the same when it perceives creation as a living reality, leading us to an organic knowledge that benefits all human life and the entire universe. This knowledge enriches us and helps us to live rightly, thus enhancing life's beauty. It was to a barefoot Moses, with his forehead pressed to the ground in utter acknowledgement of the mystery and fascination of the life drawing him toward the burning bush, that Someone revealed himself, speaking to him, calling him (cf. Ex 3:1-6).

Even inanimate objects have a personal aspect. When knowledge is used as a point of departure, creatures communicate something personal about the Creator. Inanimate objects express and transmit information about their maker and giver. But sin has damaged this principle of union and separation, which is needed for living life to the full.

Sin interferes with and damages our ability to relate, because it corrupts love. Indeed, sin is possible only because God is Love, and since love is free, it includes the possibility of rebellion, of refusal, of rejection. Sin disrupts relationships; it is isolation, a closing-off. Sin makes the self the epicenter of creation—of all things and all relationships. This leads to a tragic rupture of wholeness and harmony, obscuring one's perception of union and awareness of belonging, extinguishing the sense of community. Cordial relations are forgotten. Sin prevents us from seeing the other as a real person, free and independent from us. Sin introduces the calculations of self-interest; the other becomes an object to be used. One transforms a person into an object, and everything is objectified—faces, features, expressions, and gestures are forgotten. Sin is oblivion, and this river of oblivion swallows the dead and carries them away, making them disappear forever. Without a rapport of union and of separation in regard to what we wish to know, we cannot have accurate knowledge. In fact, sin leads to uncertainty, ignorance, and even the impossibility of knowing.

If we consider Saint Augustine's example—that at the root of memory one recognizes truth or lack of it—we can verify the connection between sin and knowledge. Sin destroys the ability to relate because it corrupts love, and at the same time it destroys the truth of the human person, one's authentic identity. Then the temptation always comes to embellish one's identity with various philosophies, convictions, and theories. But to rediscover our own truth, we need redemption from sin. We cannot free ourselves from sin nor restore what sin has destroyed. Either we will discover our truth in Christ the Redeemer, and find ourselves re-established in a healed capacity for relationship, or we will continue to create models for ourselves, ideals of ourselves upon which to base our judgments of success or failure, triumph or defeat.

Knowledge and Redeemed Relationships

> Love is the connection by which the totality of all things is
> linked together by the bonds of an inexpressible friendship
> and an indissoluble unity.[7]
>
> *John Scotus Eriugena*

We cannot know ourselves on our own. To know ourselves we must recover our ability to relate in freedom: to have with ourselves, the world, others—and even with time—a relationship that is not possessive, domineering, or exploitive. Our healthy capacity for relationship is damaged when the will has an exaggerated desire for self-assertion. We can reason and seek to establish relationships on the basis of an ethical rationality, but history shows this to be an illusion doomed to fail. Simply deciding to experience healthy relationships doesn't give us the ability to relate. A capacity for relating means that I am not the only one at stake, as a single point of reference. Relationships do not depend on me alone. Neither are there purely two-way relationships, I-you, even though some have entertained the utopian illusion that by finding one's soul mate one could create a paradise made for two. This, too, is a bitter illusion destined for a tragic end! Relationships are like a network, a tapestry unfolding through space and time, reaching down into the depths of the inexhaustible love of the triune God, the Three Persons who are truly free and faithful in their love. And such a tapestry, enfolding all humanity, can be restored only by a Person who, in the drama of sin and death, in the travail of the history of all creation, can live a love that is total, universal, and free (cf. Col 1:15–20). This is a love lived in relationship with all that exists, with all space and time, with all history. It extends to Adam and all his descendants, each person individually and, at the same time and in the same action, to all the relationships of humanity.

Redemption in Christ:
The Terrain of True Knowledge

What makes man human, the source of his humanness, is his Divine-humanity.[8]

S. Frank

The mystery of the incarnation of the Word contains within itself the meaning of all the symbols and enigmas of Scripture, and also the hidden meaning of all sensible and intelligible creation. But the one who knows the mystery of the Cross and of the Tomb also knows the fundamental reasons of all things. Finally, the one who penetrates even further and finds himself initiated into the mystery of the resurrection, learns the purpose for which God created all things in the beginning.[9]

Maximus the Confessor

This healing of relationships, so radical as to come across as a new creation, has been accomplished in Jesus Christ (cf. 2 Cor 5:17). Christ is the full revelation in history of the free and absolute love of the Persons of the Most Holy Trinity. In Christ, true God and true Man, all God's love for humanity is communicated. And Christ, the new Adam, reinforces and radiates before God all the truth and beauty of redeemed humanity (cf. 1 Cor 15:44–49). In assuming our human nature in the incarnation, Christ established an entirely unique relationship with every person. In him, every person can find access to every other person: the relationship with the other that Christ established. Christ becomes the gate (cf. Jn 10:7) through which one can enter into communion with all human beings (cf. Col 1:17). By means of his love and relationships,

Christ becomes the gate through which one can enter into communion with all human beings . . .

Christ establishes a rapport with us, absorbing and taking upon himself our condition of coldness, violence, egoism, and sin—and thus of death. All the vengeance and hatred of humanity is unleashed on him, the true victim of all the evil in the world. By taking upon himself the sins of the human race, he reconciles all men and women, showing us that the wall of division has been torn down and that suddenly we can see each another as brothers and sisters (cf. Eph 2:14–18). In taking upon himself our sins, Christ dies; since death is the wages of sin, death penetrates his flesh. But because he is the Son of God, and the Father generates and loves him from all eternity, the eternal relationship between the Father and the Son defeats death. It destroys the night with inaccessible light and raises the Son from death. Thus, in Christ the truly liberated person rises from the power of death, and sin's power is no longer definitive. The tempter is defeated. The true image of God is affirmed as love, as is the true image of the human person, which is, in some manner, the love of God. Christ, Son of God and Savior of the world, true God and true man, dead and risen, is the image in which we are able to recognize ourselves because we remember who we truly are.

With redemption, we are rehabilitated to live our self-truth—that we are persons created in the image of the triune God, the God of free and faithful relationships, that is, the God of love. These relationships are not theoretical and abstract, but concrete, personal, and historical. Christ recreates the new person, opening to him or her the possibility of loving, since Christ himself is the love through which we

Christ is the Love of the Father that touches us, that very Love through which we are able to love and to break out of ourselves.

re-enter the world of relationships. Christ is the Love of the Father that touches us, that very Love through which we are able to love and to break out of ourselves. Christ is the paradigm of all love between human beings and God, and among human beings themselves. On this bridge, so to speak, we walk toward God, thanks to the relationship God has established with us by giving us his Son, who in self-abandonment dwelt among us and remains with us. Because of this, a healthy capacity for relationships is restored to us in Christ. This capacity constitutes the starting point and context for knowledge of self, of others, and, even more, of God. Redemption is a reality so appropriate, concrete, and personal that it becomes the basis, both objective and personal, of an unforgettable memory.

The Holy Spirit and Participation in Trinitarian Love

> Since the Spirit is in the Word, it is evident that the Spirit is in God through the Word. So if the Spirit comes into us, the Son and the Father will also come and make their home in us. For the Trinity is indivisible and the divinity is one.[10]

Athanasius

As God's creation, the human person and human nature participate in the divine life and nature. Now, the essence of the divine life and nature is Love, as the Fathers of the Church repeatedly affirm. More explicitly, God's essence consists in the relationships of love among the Trinitarian Persons, who are one God. In this sense, Christian monotheism differs from other forms of monotheism. This truth has immediate consequences for understanding the concept of humanity as well as history, society, and the Church. According to revelation and the Christian tradition, the point of departure for understanding the creation of human beings is that the divine nature coincides with Love. We are created in God's image, and so we participate in God's life and truth. Clearly there is an ontological gap (or "abyss," as Saint Ephrem called it) between God and humans. Nevertheless, by the grace of God this abyss has been filled, so that it is not as deep as the one that exists between humanity and the rest of creation. In fact, humans, created persons, participate in the personal dimension of God; they are his image. This means that in our essence, even as creatures, we are what God in his essence is on an uncreated level: Love. The created person is a person precisely because of the relational core that constitutes him or her an image of God. This relational core makes the person capable of accepting relationship with God. This relationship is foundational, life-giving, and creative, as well as the source of relationships with others, the world, and the human nature that each person possesses.

In the theological sense of the term (in reference to God, but also to humans in the area of theological anthropology), the person cannot be reduced to a mere subject. Each man and woman is composed, so to speak, of a dimension that is affectionate, spiritual, absolutely personal, and unrepeatable, inseparably united to what we call "human nature," which is common to all of us. Thus, there is within the person an irreplaceable dimension that comes from the gift of love received in creation and redemption. But this irreplaceable dimension is realized not only on the personal level, but also through and in the nature that all humans share. In itself, human nature does not tell us much about an individual, but rather about the species, about the human race in general. Human nature takes on a personal face, an unmistakable dimension, only by allowing itself to be penetrated by the love that God gives to each one of us, so that we become an unrepeatable and unique person. The dimension of love enters into human nature as the power to freely establish relationships; thus, human nature is transformed through love. In relationships a person achieves his or her completeness. And it is there that the inseparability of the two dimensions of a human being may be seen. Loving and relating always imply the action of the gift of love received from the Holy Spirit. But this action works primarily on the individual's human nature. For this reason, every act of love also means loving oneself. We find personal fulfillment in relationships that simultaneously include our own nature, the world, others, and God. By relating lovingly with others, we also relate with our own nature. By loving others, we love ourselves, and vice versa. Rapport with another includes and engages our own nature. In this way, while love among persons is indeed intersubjective, it also includes

Every act of love also means loving oneself.

the objective aspect of human nature. A human person may be viewed as a relational reality that is complex, not merely intersubjective.

Understood in this way, relationship cannot be reduced to a simple rapport between two subjects, precisely because relationship pertains to the reality of the person, who includes within him or herself that objective principle constituted by human nature. But neither can relations, understood in this way, be reduced to the simple world of psychology, because the reality in their core is theological, and thus clearly spiritual. The ability to relate, then, has its origin in the Trinitarian world. Any attempt to confine relationships solely within a socio-psychological analysis is a deceptive form of reductionism that hinders a true understanding of relationships, and therefore also of the individual and society. Such an approach often leads to an interpretation of the capacity to relate that cannot open itself to the true origin of relationships, namely the Trinitarian world.

If we consider the human person as the image of God, we see that the One who communicates the divine life, the One who makes the created person a participant in God's nature, is the Holy Spirit. It is the Spirit who descends first, who, in this sense, lives his kenosis. The Spirit dwells in the creature, and by this action transforms him or her as a person, because the Spirit implants agape, which is constituted by participation in God the Father. The Holy Spirit impresses upon the soul of the new creature—which is the human being's personal realm—his image, which is the image of the Son. In Christian symbolism "image" signifies the real and active presence of the Son. And as the Son is the image of the Father (cf. Col 1:15), the Father, too, is made present. Thus, the human creature receives in his or her person a Trinitarian imprint. The Holy Spirit makes us sharers in God's life, uniting us to the divine life, disclosing to us the Love that exists among the Persons of the Trinity, drawing us into the Trinitarian Love. We can therefore say that the human person is created in the image of God the Father, the Son, and the Holy Spirit, and that our essence as human persons is both our relationship with the triune God who creates, vivifies, saves, and sanctifies, and our acceptance of this truth—the living out of the same reality of relationship and love.

Our Union with the New Adam

Born of a virgin and pierced in your side, O my Creator, having become Adam you refashioned Eve. Sleeping super-naturally in a life-giving slumber, in your almighty power you reawakened life from sleep and from the flesh. . . . The

spotless temple has been destroyed, but the fallen taberna-
cle has been raised with you. The second Adam, who dwells
in the highest heavens, has descended to the first Adam, to
the uttermost chambers of Hades.[11]

Troparion for Byzantine Orthros

It was by the Holy Spirit that the Word became incarnate
in the Virgin of Nazareth. The Holy Spirit is the architect of
the incarnation and, therefore, of the complete manifestation
of God. At one and the same time this is the redemption of
man and woman, the manifestation of God's glory on the face
of Christ, and the contemplation thereon of our redemption.
Thanks to the Holy Spirit, we can recognize Christ as our Lord
and intuit the depths of the sacrificial and saving love between
the Father and the Son. Thus we discover that we are loved by
God in his Son—whom we recognize as both Savior and
brother—because it is the Spirit himself who makes us sons
and daughters in the Son, and utters within us the true name
of God, which is "Father."

It is the Spirit who, communicating to us our redemption
by Christ, the work of salvation, and the revelation of God as
Father, reveals our true identity as God's children (cf. Rm
8:14–17). The Holy Spirit brings us back to the Father through
Christ, the Son of God, who took the form of a slave and suf-
fered the humiliations of those enslaved by sin and passion in
order to restore our lost sonship. And through the Spirit we
contemplate on the face of the Son of God, become a slave,
the filial imprint with which the Consoler identified us at our
creation. The Spirit shows us that in Christ, the new Adam,
the complete reality of the original creation is rediscovered. In

fact, Christ, the new Adam, recapitulates and reintegrates everything of Adam and his descendants. The Holy Spirit gives us eyes to see that the new Adam takes upon himself all the failure, deceit, betrayal, sin, and death of the old Adam (cf. Phil 2:7). Everything that once existed without love is assumed and consumed by the Father's love, so that it can shine forth transfigured and revealed as God's true and perfect image.

Charity: The Enduring Reality

> By taking flesh, the Word associated himself with man and took upon himself our nature, so that the human person could be deified, without confusion with God: the fabric of our nature is completely sanctified by Christ, the first fruits of creation.[12]
>
> *Gregory of Nyssa*

How can we accept redemption? How can we participate in it? From our viewpoint as creatures, the Holy Spirit, who according to Saint Augustine is the Love of the Love of God, pours into our hearts the love of God the Father (cf. Rm 5:5). He is the communicator of God's life—that is, of his love. He is the supreme Gift of the Father, but for us the Spirit is also the Giver. Since time immemorial, Christians have recognized the Holy Spirit as the divine Person who dwells within humans through his action. And, since apostolic times, this action has been recognized first of all as the communication of love, of charity, as shown in the example of Saint Stephen, who was "full of faith and the Holy Spirit" (Acts 6:5) to the point of giving his life. The Holy Spirit dwells in us through holy charity, which is agape perceived and lived in creation and history. For this reason, charity is the only enduring reality, for it unifies everything, even opposites. Holy charity remains because it is so divine that it can bear rejection, rebellion, and opposition. Charity allows itself to be trampled upon, humiliated, destroyed—as did Christ, who is the manifestation of the Father's love—but it always revives. It remains humble, meek, without self-interest, without the desire for self-assertion, without the desire to possess its own space, its own form of existence. Charity is eternal life. Charity embraces so much of who God is—Love—that nothing created can destroy it. Even in the darkest recesses of history, the charity poured forth by the Holy Spirit preserves a continuous openness toward the fathomless depths of the Triune God's personal love.

Charity lives on two levels—one exposed to history, time, sin, and violence; the other to the faithfulness of the Triune God. One is bound to the flesh and to the insecurity of creatures, while the other is linked to inaccessible light, lasting happiness, and the fullness of the Trinitarian encounter. So one level is sunk in the tragedy of sin, exposed to the violence of sin's mentality, and the other basks in the steadfast faithfulness of God the Father, Son, and Holy Spirit. Jesus Christ, true God and true man, incarnate by the power of the Holy Spirit, is the absolute fulfillment of this polarity of love between the created and uncreated. And the Lord's Passover is the foundation and summit of everything that occurs between death and eternal life, between sin and inaccessible light, between fickleness and faithful encounter, between sadness and joy. Charity is, therefore, also a passage, a passover, an exodus from the old Adam to the new. Charity weaves all of history into a single tapestry. Because it endures forever, charity preserves all that truly remains. And its way of remaining is the way of passage. Anything that does not enter into the Paschal mystery is not of charity, and so it does not remain. What enters into the Easter Triduum endures: dying out of love, being buried, and being raised on the third day by the Holy Spirit, as revealed to us in Christ, our Passover.

Charity is . . . therefore, also a passage, a passover, an exodus from the old Adam to the new.

The Holy Spirit guides everything to Christ. The Spirit is forever the One who incarnates the Son, who makes Christ historical and eternally present, as in the celebration of the sacred liturgy.

Together with the gift of charity, the Holy Spirit also gives us the gift of intelligence and memory. Charity is the highest form of intelligence. It is the light of the intellect because it sees everything in relation to everything else. Charity is the connecting fabric. Spiritual authors used to speak of an illuminated charity, of a discreet charity—that is, a charity that discerns and comprehends. Such charity promotes the highest form of intelligence, which shows the truth of each detail in its relationship to everything else, connecting the particular to the whole. And since everything that allows itself to be penetrated by charity endures forever, charity coincides with memory. Memory is therefore closely linked with the Holy Spirit, the Giver of charity. In the anthropological sense, the source of memory is the Holy Spirit and his gift of charity. Memory is intrinsically connected to intelligence and life, because the Holy Spirit is the Lord and giver of life, since he communicates the love of God the Father. The human person therefore possesses an intellectual structure that has charity as its foundation and the Holy Spirit as its vital principle. And as its sphere of awareness, this structure has the experience of persons in relationship with God, with others, with themselves, and with all creation.

The Divine Life-giving Memory

The good thief prays from the Cross: "Remember me, O Lord, when you come into your kingdom." He asks to be remembered. And in response, Jesus Christ grants his wish and affirms: "Truly I tell you, today you will be with me in paradise" (Lk 23:42–43). In other words, "being remembered" by the Lord is the same as "being in paradise," and this means being in the eternal memory and, in consequence, having eternal existence and eternal remembrance in God.[13]

Pavel A. Florenskij

By means of charity, the Holy Spirit urges every human person toward Christ that he or she may become a daughter or son in the Son. The Spirit reveals the meaning of this divine filiation to each of us and reminds us of it continually. By communicating to us God's life and Christ's salvation, the Spirit makes the image of our identity concrete. The Spirit makes us share in the filial dimension of our existence from the moment of our creation, and then makes personal to each of us the redemption accomplished by Christ. In this way the Holy Spirit continually enlivens within us the reality of the image, which thus becomes a spiritual reminder of our truth. Through the charity poured out on us and through divine participation, the Spirit calls forth from us those genuine and efficacious recollections that constitute our spiritual memory. He causes every person to remember what he or she is becoming, is called to be. This spiritual memory opens our inner eyes to our goal, our fulfillment, which has already been realized for each of us in the Passover of Christ. By its nature, the spiritual memory that is communicated to us is a created entity. So it is found where the world of the spirit meets the world of the psyche. But in the world of God, the personal memory of the three divine Persons is an absolute act of thought and creation. God remembers, and this coincides with an act of blessing and protection toward the reality remembered. Thus, God's memory is his presence, his faithful companionship. In fact, Scripture reveals God's memory as a permanent, constant act of fidelity toward that which is remembered. God's memory is a type of covenant, the permanence of his "being with" us: he is Emanuel, God-with the remembered (cf. Ps 11:5).

> **God's memory is a type of covenant, the permanence of his "being with" us: he is Emanuel, God-with the remembered.**

The Grasping Human Memory

You should say to the moment: "But stay, You are so
beautiful!"[14]

J. W. Goethe

In the psychological and, therefore, the created world, the
memory can render things present. Even in our thoughts, our
memory can make images and concepts present through the
act of remembering. But it is specifically at the psychological
level that the memory's characteristic of "recalling" becomes
evident as it tries to hold on to things, to keep them from dis-
appearing. This tendency can reach the point of pathological
nostalgia, which can become a type of psychological block. A
person becomes so attached to the past that he or she cannot
let it go. Since it is impossible to revive the past—to bring it
into the present—one tries to convert the present into the past.
This type of nostalgia bleeds the memory dry.

In a way, we can understand the memory's desire to make
reality present. We can even understand the pathology of nostalgia, so closely connected to the deepest, primordial wound in
our memory, constituted by sin. Sin completely changes the
backdrop of our lives because it radically alters a person's very
identity—a catastrophe so grave that a person recognizes that his
or her previous reality no longer exists. So the person turns to
the past, longing for its return. The illness of nostalgia is chiefly
spiritual. It affects the whole person: one's psyche and ability to
reason, as evidenced in human history. This is always true of
efforts to recover experiences, situations, surroundings. . . .
Basically, nostalgia links memory and recollections with certain

cultural, psychological, social, and political models. For this reason, it represents attachment to an objectified reality, interwoven more or less consciously with the search for a lost pleasure, a security that has vanished, a life one no longer has.

Even if nostalgia seems to seek certain persons or relationships, it is in some way an egotistical search. Our ego wants to recover what gave it security, pleasure, enjoyment, and self-affirmation. Consequently, nostalgia does not allow for progress, nor does it accept internal or external changes in others. Nostalgia freezes us in the past. We have all experienced nostalgia for someone only to be bitterly disappointed when we met that person again, because he or she was not who we remembered. Isn't this proof that we were more attached to our idea of the person than to a real relationship with him or her? Nostalgia hardens the memory. And this hardening is the result of the dichotomy between charity, and the tendency to objectify everything—to transform objects, ideas, and feelings into possessions. The mentality of sin expands the rupture caused by sin. We see this tendency in a nostalgia that leads to a connection between faces and things, persons and objects, personal relationships and sentiments and ideas—not on the basis of charity, and, therefore, not on the basis of paschal agape.

Also from the moral aspect, flaws are found in the way that a hardened memory and nostalgic reasoning process engage the human will. In trying to regain a lost perfection, we set up models to which we must conform. This artificial approach, disconnected from life, ends in unhappiness. Such an approach may lead to sacrifice, renunciation, self-improvement, and education. But it brings no enjoyment of life, no delight in the experience of personal growth. Such a pursuit of perfection is disconnected from love. It reflects the fragments of an illusory unity that is never attained. Simply put, one part has been taken for the whole. This process results in idealizing the memory and basing one's reasoning on recollections that are imagined or constructed and, therefore, are not memory at all.

Joyous Remembrance

Nostalgia involves suffering because the past is absent. Anamnesis is a joyous remembrance that makes the past more present than it was when experienced.[15]

T. Spidlik

Only a memory that recalls the Paschal Mystery is a living memory. This memory assures us of wisdom regarding how to live so as to not endure lasting death, how to live with all illusions unmasked. To remember the paschal event is to know that all things return not as they were once experienced, but transformed. They are transfigured in the process of redemption, which is the process of universal filiation in Christ. This is not nostalgia because it is recovery in Christ for the Father, in whose house all things are regained, as they were for the prodigal son (cf. Lk 15:11–32). Whatever the prodigal son regains in his father's house is not the same as what he squandered. Everything is changed because it is transformed into the story of the father's love. The father makes himself present as care and concern for his son, as the love that awaits his son and celebrates their encounter. The spiritual memory makes everything present through the transfiguration of the Paschal

Mystery. It recovers everything because it remembers all in relation to the Paschal Mystery—that is, in relation to a God who communicates himself to us in a paschal manner. And the Paschal Mystery does away with every rigid, nostalgic, formalistic, possessive thought.

In the Church's tradition the word *anamnesis* indicates the memory that has the Holy Spirit as its vital principle, which weaves memories into a lasting tapestry of charity. In fact, on the level of created things, memory culminates in the creative and life-giving outlet of the liturgy, where it is transformed into *anamnesis*. The liturgy is the only place wherein the human memory, which through participation possesses the desire to create and to retain, achieves this profound characteristic. In the liturgy, the human memory is united so effectively and

> **In the liturgy, the human memory is united so effectively and entirely to God's memory as to make present what is remembered.**

entirely to God's memory as to actually make present what is remembered. The work of the Holy Spirit is to "render present," and this is fulfilled in the liturgy. In fact, *anamnesis* is accompanied by *epiclesis*. Without the invocation of the Holy Spirit (*epiclesis*), our memory remains powerless. It either dissolves into oblivion, dying with those things that pass away, or hardens into nostalgia. In the liturgy, on the contrary, memory enters into *anamnesis*. With ecclesial wisdom—that is, with the rationality of combined thought, and therefore with the intelligence of love— memory recognizes the objectivity of Christ celebrated as Lord and Savior. Throughout history, Christ ceaselessly reveals the Father and to redeem us from the slavery of sin. With its ecclesial wisdom, the liturgy nourishes the recollections of our spiritual memory, which is open to *anamnesis*, to eternal memory.

In the liturgy, memory nourishes and is nourished by the entire spiritual complexity of the Church—the Word of God, symbols, dogmas, concepts, metaphors, spiritual meanings and images, the practice of charity. . . . Thus, the memory of salvation—the memory of Christ, true God and true man— embedded in these realities of the Church, continually vivifies our participation through Christ in the love of the Father. Memory is participation. It is effective participation in the gift of God. For this reason, the memory of Christ and salvation transforms our mentality. It continually corrects our own memory, so that we can recognize what is and is not of Christ. It also makes us recognize what is and is not our own identity as sons and daughters in the Son. The memory of Christ and salvation transforms the way we live and our moral activity, because it continually nourishes us with the memory of the Paschal Mystery as the only path of human fulfillment. Fulfillment is not reached abstractly or in isolation, but within a relationship with the paschal Christ communicated to us by the Holy Spirit.

Unity: Guarantee of Life

The more you unify your heart in the search for him, the more he is constrained by his compassion and by his goodness to come to you and repose in you. . . . And when he

sees your zeal in seeking him, then he will manifest himself
and will appear to you. He will grant you his help and will
give you victory, freeing you from your enemies. When he
sees, above all, how you seek him and how you always place
all of your hope in him, then he will teach you, he will give
you the gift of true prayer, of the true charity that is himself,
and he will become everything for you: paradise, tree of life,
pearl, crown, builder, farmer . . . man and God, wine, living
water, sheep, bridegroom, warrior, armor, Christ who is all
in all.[16]

                                                    Pseudo-Macarius

To examine ourselves means to see ourselves in relation to
the Prototype. This practice helps us to increase our self-knowledge in relation to what we are called to be and, therefore, to
see ourselves always more integrally. But we must clarify what
this means. Personal unification does not simply mean perfection according to a projected ideal. Our relationship with our
Creator and Redeemer integrates us. We feel ourselves
embraced by the loving gaze of the Redeemer, who unites our
entire person, our history, and our future. Unless integration
is understood in this way, we cannot carry out an examination
of conscience, because we do not know what to refer to when
examining ourselves. If we don't know that, we again risk stray-
ing into depersonalizing categories, abstractions, and moralism.
Let us try, then, to uncover the meaning of spiritual unity as
personal integration.

The principle of life is union, while the tendency to isolate
oneself is the source of death. Everything that distances itself,
that closes itself off, that seeks supremacy, ends up dying. In
creation, the origin of life is marked by union and by

relationship. Life is transmitted through relationships, while death triumphs by cutting them off. Sin has deceived human beings by promising that if each of us is self-centered, and if we run our lives totally the way we want, we will survive and succeed. But this deception from the tempter has dug humanity's graveyard. Wounded by sin, bleeding because our self-imposed solitude has severed relationships, we search for salvation by centering on ourselves. This is a possessive way of relating. We seek security by exploiting our relationships and the pleasing things that we acquire to maintain life. Such possessiveness, incapable of true relationship, creates ivory towers and ideological systems to make one feel powerful, alive, and invulnerable. Strangely enough, on the psychological level, all this leads to satisfaction—but only to satisfaction. To be happy is quite another matter. Sooner or later, those who are only satisfied will grow bored by the very things they sought.

In fact, the satisfaction that sin lures us into is a camouflaged form of dissatisfaction. It is bitterness and defeat. In this regard the Russian philosopher Vladimir Solovyov speaks of the philosophical concept of "evil infinity"—the wounded person's hunger. This hunger is never satisfied because his or her life is self-centered. Such a desire is an unquenchable thirst, an unattainable longing for self-assertion. The person can no longer see any boundaries, because everything that once gave pleasure and satisfaction eventually brings boredom or even bitterness. One loses oneself in everything that was amassed to save oneself. Like the prodigal son, a person accumulates things in order to manage and enjoy them according to his or her own will. Paradoxically, the same things that should bring satisfaction end up enslaving the person. He or she begins to fall apart interiorly because of so many increasingly anxious, agitated, insatiable desires. This is the demon that is called legion, because it is manifold (cf. Mk 5:9). It brings disintegration. It deceives us into thinking that every part, if satisfied, can absorb the whole and placate the desire to be. It is a true demonic illusion. One falls prey to divisions, to separations, to fragmentation. It becomes impossible to understand oneself as a totality. And so the person looks at him or herself in a broken mirror, with a sorrow and a suffering that is already a form of death.

Happiness is found in unity, because unity guarantees life. Life is guaranteed only in a union that does not exclude anyone. If even a part is excluded—that is, pushed into isolation, where it nurtures rancor and aggression—it eventually becomes a threat to all, as well as to itself. The true guarantee of life is communion with everyone. This communion considers and engages all; at the same time it does not use violence nor does it injure by crowding. By affirming all, it is able to affirm each. This and only this is a life of security and well-being that a person can experience as happiness. We discover this criterion within ourselves, even before we see it on a social level: we live our identity, our truth. We find serenity and peace only if we live our own unity, if we look at ourselves in such a way as to see ourselves completely, that is, integrally.

Seeing Ourselves Completed in Christ

What is the true way that the Scripture calls "the narrow road that leads to life" (Mt 7:14), "the way of peace" (Lk 1:79), "a way of salvation" (Acts 16:17), "the Way" (Acts 19:9), "the way of truth" (2 Pet 2:2) and "the straight road"

(2 Pet 2:15)? It is purity-chastity. In Russian, the etymology of the word refers to completeness, health, wholeness, unity, and in general the normal state of the interior life, the person's wholeness and strength, the freshness of spiritual energies, the spiritual harmony of the inner person. It is practically the same thing as integrity of thought, of reason, of the intellect—the well-being of reason and intellect. This is exactly the meaning of the term that was used by the Holy Fathers and the ancient philosophers. It is simplicity, which means organic unity, and if one wishes, the integrity of the person.[17]

Pavel A. Florenskij

To see ourselves completely means to see the connections among our different dimensions—reason, intellect, intuition, will, emotions, senses, body, passions, instincts, etc. It means to see our continuity through the years, in the present and through time. We see the connections of our personal identity through all the events and parts of our lives. Cultural connections are also woven into our identity: geographical background, skin color, genetic structure—that is, bonds with parents and ancestors. There are also links between reality and dreams, desires and projects, successes and failures. Seeing ourselves completely means keeping in mind the entire spectrum of our relationships, encounters, and surroundings.

Instinctively, we see that the mystery of joy and happiness is found in unity. For this reason, we often want to overcome personal disintegration by our own efforts. We try to reintegrate our lives by means of abstract mental criteria or categories, seeking to recover certain images within us or to adapt to certain forms. But, as we have seen, there is no unifying principle except the reality of Trinitarian love. The love of God is the seamless fabric that supports, sustains, and actualizes the person's reality. This means entering into the perspective of love—regarding ourselves, understanding ourselves, and growing in the light of love. In this way we become more completely integrated.

Often a trap lurks: we cannot love ourselves on our own, unaided. We need to *discover* that we are loved. Love is a surprise; otherwise, it is not love. We cannot force others to love us. Love is a gift of the Holy Spirit. And the realization of love within us, of the recapitulation of the whole person in love, is the redemption carried out by Christ and given to us in the Spirit. In order to see ourselves in truth, we must look at ourselves with the eyes of the Holy Spirit, which is also the gaze of Christ the Savior. It is the mercy of God. To see ourselves in reality and truth, we must ask for this gift from the Holy Spirit, who leads us back to Christ. Only Jesus can tell us how we appear, because he looks at us and does not hesitate to give his very life to restore our own.

Wisdom: Ambient of Communication with God

Although the only-begotten and primordial Wisdom of God creates and constructs everything . . . in order that what is created should not only exist, but should exist in a worthy manner, it pleased God that his Wisdom should descend to creatures; so that all of his creatures in general and individually should be marked with a sort of seal and likeness of his own image, and so that what had been brought into being should show itself as wisely made and worthy of God. Since, then, there exists in us and in all things this seal of created Wisdom, the true and creative Wisdom, identifying with what is said of his own seal, says of himself: "The Lord created me among his works." The same Lord in a certain sense calls upon what could be called the Wisdom existing in us, and although as Creator he was not himself created, nevertheless because of his created image in things he says this, as it were, of himself. The Lord himself said: "Whoever welcomes you welcomes me" (Mt 10:40). Since his seal is in us, then, although he is not counted among created things, but his image and likeness have been created in things, he speaks as though he were himself this image: "The Lord created me at the beginning of his work, the first of his acts of long ago, before his works." As I have said, the seal of Wisdom has been impressed upon things so that in the wisdom of its creator the world may recognize the Word, and through the Word, the Father. . . . The creative Wisdom is not in the world, but rather the created wisdom within things, on account of which "The heavens are telling the glory of God; and the firmament proclaims his handiwork" (Ps 19:1). If people also welcome this wisdom within themselves, they will recognize the true wisdom of God; they will recognize that they have truly been created in the image of God.[18]

Athanasius

This place of encounter between divine and human, between uncreated and created, between absolute and fragile—this loving gaze of our Creator and Savior—is preserved for us and communicated to us in the Wisdom of God. Wisdom is the vision that God had when he created us. Wisdom was present at the time of creation (cf. Prov 8:30), and therefore knows the works of God (cf. Wis 9:9). Wisdom reminds us of the meaning and destiny of all things, watching over the life of all. In divine Wisdom, God preserves all the truly existing images and ideas of everything that he creates in love and redeems in his Son. Wisdom is therefore the ambient that God provides for us through the Holy Spirit so that created persons can communicate with God. Wisdom is the loving intelligence communicated to created beings in order to nourish our memory with the real and active memory of God. It is a meeting place where we can contemplate ourselves through God's eyes and can remember ourselves as the Spirit remembers us, as we were created, as Christ redeemed us. And we can hear what he is saying to us.

Vision of the Holy Spirit

The Holy Spirit is the charity that beckons.[19]

William of Saint-Thierry

Divine Wisdom is the intelligible and living reality that allows us to develop a way of thinking according to criteria and categories related to life. Reasoning that takes wisdom as its starting point deals with concepts and ideas infused with life. The result, then, is not simply a system of thought; this approach avoids the risk of ideology. Thought based on the premises of divine Wisdom creates a body of concepts, notions, and ideas that is a living organism.

Divine Wisdom is a gift; it is the charity of God toward human beings. It is the Lord's act of teaching, filled with his tenderness for us and given in order to protect us from mere theorizing. This gift enables us to contemplate the mysteries of humanity, life, history, and God himself according to the way of wisdom, which is always united to enduring and undying life. This way of thinking prevents us from getting lost in abstract theories about human beings (our intelligence, soul, psyche, and history), about the cosmos, and about God.

Theories are often based on ideas that are disconnected from life or at least do not take into account life in its entirety—above all, the personal life that includes the mystery of the free formation of relationships. Theories often spring from a desire to dominate, to establish mastery over mystery. They easily stem from a grasping, sensual, possessive way of reasoning based on illusion, on the serpent's temptation in Genesis 3. Such theories fence life in, imprison it, isolate it, and become more important than life itself. For this reason, such theories are in constant conflict with human love, human freedom, and the events of human history. And because they produce rigid methodologies applied mechanically, they even enslave human beings. Nothing must oppose their enforcement. Thought that is driven by passion, thought that establishes a bond between reason and passion, permits a possessive culture that tends to domination. Such an attitude often disguises itself behind abstract approaches, as if to make these abstract notions seem disconnected from the passions, to guarantee that they are the result of impartial reasoning, to show that they avoid possessiveness. Instead, all systems of thought that start from abstract, theoretical assumptions sooner or later become a technique that causes a reversal: technology itself becomes a system of thought.

In a world of technocracy, of the massive diffusion of new technologies, the human person might become so dominated that he or she must correspond to the vision favored by technology. This means that humanity could be transformed so radically by technology's impact on human nature that a "new" person would result. There is little doubt that this is our future. And there seems to be little benefit in opposing it with "humanistic," ethical, moral theories, or by taking legal action. With the current world order—driven by economic and financial interests that effectively enlist human passions, desires for self-assertion, and the search for pleasure—it is impossible to create effective opposition by using a system of thought based solely on alternative ethical-moral values.

> **We need to promote a culture of thinking, reflecting, and creating that is not detached from love.**

It might be more effective to develop a way of thinking based on wisdom that would foster an organic reasoning. This wisdom, if it were to develop notions and concepts, would be based on human life in a context of relationships, a communitarian context characterized by a specific way of living. We need to promote a culture of thinking, reflecting, and creating that is not detached from love. Only this could serve as a successful antidote to the enormous pathological development of technocratic reasoning, which has now become a danger for humanity. This culture could foster a harmonious way of thinking and living that would be beautiful, joyful, and, therefore, attractive. We can only safeguard the future of our race if we start from the point of beauty understood as spiritual unity—as a world, a thought, a reality penetrated by love and, therefore, by a life of communion.

Wisdom Dwells in Beauty

Because it proceeds from the ego and has its fulcrum in the ego, the spiritual life is truth; when perceived as the immediate action of the other, it is goodness; when objectively contemplated by a third party as an external manifestation, it is beauty. The truth manifests itself as love. Love realized is beauty.[20]

Pavel A. Florenskij

Divine Wisdom is that tapestry of beauty in which the truth reveals itself as love. And love is not an ethical imperative, an idealistic or romantic dream. It is a reality actualized in the specific face of Christ, true God and true man. It is in divine Wisdom that human beings can contemplate and approach aspects of the truth, perceived as beauty that attracts and fascinates, revealing an infinite tapestry of relationships and interconnections. In divine Wisdom, in this fascinating beauty that approaches us, draws us to itself, and reveals itself, we can contemplate the unity of all things in Christ, and in him we can contemplate our own unity. In the Paschal Mystery, Christ completely restores the old Adam. Christ reveals him as light and beauty in the wholeness constituted by the new Adam. In the Paschal Mystery, all the darkness, shortcomings, hollowness, emptiness, everything experienced in relation to the principle of self-assertion—in deception, illusion, and death—is rediscovered, illuminated, cleansed, restored, and absorbed by Christ, God and man. What was bloodied now shines like the snow in the sun. What was soiled now gleams with a whiteness bleach could never produce. In the Paschal sacrifice, beauty is realized in the true sense of the word. In the love that Christ engenders through his passover, unity is established within the world and between the world and God. The Wisdom that leads to life in beauty is the Wisdom of the Easter Triduum.

Where is this Wisdom found? Divine Wisdom is God's personal companion, with him since the beginning of creation (cf. Wis 9:9; Prov 3:19). When God created the universe, Wisdom was already with him, and God created together with Wisdom (cf. Prov 8:27). This is a fascinating, dialogic, personal aspect of God. It is an aspect that is joyous, cheerful, and festive. It is an aspect of *agape*, of love, of God's outpouring, of his desire to give. It has the characteristic of divine joy that invites and prepares banquets where encounters take place (cf. Prov 8:30; 9:2). It is God's nearness, a sort of dwelling place for God, so marked by evidence of the dweller that everything brings to mind that Person, every detail is directly linked with the renowned Inhabitant. Wisdom is the intelligible companion of God, capable of presenting itself in the form of a privileged artisan (cf. Prov 8:30). It is the artist who finds meaning in creating whatever charms and engages the creature's senses and intelligence.

Wisdom is God's vision, his idea of creation. This vision always remains within God, but it is also present in creation. Divine Wisdom is a reality with two levels: on the one hand, it belongs to God and, as the Scripture says, it is part of the uncreated world (cf. Prov 8:23); on the other hand, because it is the expression of the abundance of God's love, it is poured out by him into the created world (cf. Prov 8:24) and lives in every person who accepts the offer to become God's son or daughter. Divine Wisdom accompanies God the Creator and pervades everything that is created. In this sense, it becomes the means by which the world can access God, his thought and his plan for creation. It can be said that Wisdom preserves within itself the "original" of creation, the memory of how the created world emerged

Wisdom preserves the memories of how our Creator and Savior sees us . . .

from the hands of the Creator. Because uncreated Wisdom is the ambient of communication among the divine Persons, the ambient of the Love of the Trinitarian Persons, its fundamental characteristic is communication. In fact, Wisdom communicates itself in creation, and, on the level of creatures, it clothes creation in the fascination of love, communicability, and beauty.

Wisdom in the Church

Salvation lies in being one with the Church, but access to the superior, supernatural unity of creatures joined by the power of the grace of the Holy Spirit is possible only to the humble person who has purified her or himself by ascesis.

Humility, chastity, and simplicity are the transphysical and transmoral powers that, in the Holy Spirit, render the entire creature one with the Church. These powers are revelations of another world within this earthly world, of the spiritual world within the spatial-temporal world; they are the guardian angels of the creature, who descend from heaven and ascend from creation to heaven, as revealed to the patriarch Jacob, and, if we want to continue with the comparison, the "ladder" is the Most Holy Mother of God.[21]

Pavel A. Florenskij

In the normal course of things, faith is received from someone else; we cannot baptize ourselves. Thus, people normally depend upon each other for the attainment of their supernatural destiny. They are called to participate in the same good of divine life, receiving the beginning of this from someone else. In this it is possible to see a reflection of the divine life itself, which is the gift of one Person to another.[22]

Y. M. Congar

With the incarnation, death, and resurrection of Christ, and the event of Pentecost, Wisdom opens the Trinitarian world to man. This openness was formerly accessible only by intuition. Now it becomes a concrete possibility for us, and the Church becomes the privileged place of Wisdom. The wisdom of the Old Testament, through the power of the Holy Spirit, converged in the Virgin of Nazareth, the Mother of God. So now the same Spirit, in generating the Church, stirs up the Wisdom concentrated within it. The Church becomes the place where the two levels of Wisdom meet, creating this intelligible, vibrant, and beautiful tapestry that characterizes God's dwelling place: the relationships between Father, Son, and Holy Spirit. Since Wisdom is the reality in which the divine and human converge and unite, then Christ, the God-man, is Wisdom par excellence. Wisdom, then, is also his body, the Church, and within it all the persons who live their call to divinization: the Mother of God, John, the precursor, the saints. . . . And the primordial meaning of life, death, birth, suffering, joy are revealed in the Church.

Divine Wisdom takes on a visibility in the Church that prevents any misunderstanding of the mysteries through confusion or relativism. Divine Wisdom is Christocentric. It is transmitted and manifested in Scripture, in the creeds, in dogma. It has enveloped the Church's prayers, songs, and liturgy through space and time, beginning with the apostles and down through the ages. Wisdom makes itself accessible in the saints, who remain alive and glorified in Christ and who live in the communion of the Church, transcending time's boundaries. Wisdom communicates itself in the teaching that the Church's shepherds present as the wealth of the ecclesial patrimony for the world's salvation and its acceptance by the people of God. And all of the fascination and beauty of the cosmos, of the earth, of the fields, of the trees, converge and participate in the mysteries of the sacraments celebrated by the Church.

Examining Our Hearts with Wisdom

If the heart is the center of the human person, then it is through the heart that a human being enters into relationship with all that exists.[23]

Theophane the Recluse

We attain Wisdom—this unified vision—through the heart, understood as the totality of the person and the center of his or her meaning: the locus of love. The heart possesses inward energies for attracting and uniting, and outgoing energies for relating and giving. The heart is love. The heart can grasp all the connections that constitute the person in his or her entirety, while it preserves the relationships between a person and others—above all with the triune God. To see ourselves in our totality, we need to look at ourselves with our hearts. This is another way of saying that the foundation of a human being is God's love. Love is intelligibility precisely because it is communication and communion. For this reason, only love is authentic intelligence; in it are rooted all our capacities for knowledge and from it develop these same capacities: reasoning, intellect, intuition, will, emotions, senses. They are linked to love, rooted in love, and enlivened by love. In this way, each of the capacities for knowledge acts in harmony with the others, because in love each draws upon the organic connections that unite them all. Only in this way can a person grow integrally in his or her understanding, which involves the whole person and is therefore beneficial for the present life and for life everlasting.

If the heart is the meaning of the whole, the source of *agape*, it is a living reality. It can have access to Wisdom, because Wisdom communicates both understanding and life. The heart prevents the unilateral development of any single human dimension. It makes itself felt every time we overemphasize an isolated aspect, even if it is "spiritual." Because it is the guarantor of unity, the heart suffers whenever we do violence to some part of ourselves. Thus, the heart guarantees that the mind does not become disconnected from life, from love. The "intelligence of the heart"—a typical expression of spiritual writers—acts in the light of love. And love always creates unity between understanding and our spiritual life, the life that fosters our salvation.

Thus, the heart and Wisdom are two closely connected realities acting in a perfect mutual exchange. Wisdom preserves the memories of how our Creator and Savior sees us, and the heart can understand and contemplate this image, reflect on these memories, and hold on to them. Divine Wisdom preserves the memory of those spiritual recollections that become the criteria for recognizing what is truly beneficial in life, so that the Holy Spirit can strengthen our relationship as daughters and sons in the Son.

Only in the heart's unified vision can we integrate the images of the memory—the recollections of who we are according to the divine vocation. This forms a sense of the unity of the living organism, of love. This sense of the heart and of the wisdom that fosters, preserves, and actualizes genuine human life, can be equated with "conscience." Conscience is that watchful voice that makes itself heard every time we experience something that concerns these realities. This sense of love as the most personal and the most universal reality is the inner unity expressed in and through the uniqueness of the conscience, the personal "I."

In summary: only love is truly communicable and intelligible. Only the love of the triune God is eternal life, in which relationships remain forever. At the moment of our creation, the Holy Spirit communicates this love to us, which dwells within us as holy charity, as light. The mystery of our personal unity and our happiness is preserved in this love. Sin destroys the person, distorting love into an exaggerated egoism, but redemption by Christ heals us. It recreates the new person, and the Holy Spirit enables us to participate in this salvation by causing us to live as daughters and sons in the Son. In his love for human beings, God reveals his mysteries through his Wisdom, which can communicate to us understanding and life in the same action. The Church preserves the holy memory, the Wisdom of the redeemed person who lives in Christ. We grow by contemplating with our heart our true image preserved in the Church by divine Wisdom and communicated to us by the Holy Spirit, who makes a gift of this love to us. With the heart's intelligence, we can draw on memory for the criteria to discern what helps or harms our position as children in the Son, living as redeemed persons as history unfolds.

So when I examine my conscience, I perform an act of prayer. Calling on the Holy Spirit and activating my heart's intelligence, which is the vision of the whole, I contemplate my life—attitudes, actions, thoughts, feelings, decisions, relationships. I do this against the background of memory and the precise recollections of how Christ in his paschal love sees me. I seek to see myself as Christ saw me during his Paschal Mystery, when he redeemed me. This means seeing myself within the memory of Christ. His memory of me as a redeemed person is my truth and the true image of my person. Then, as Saint Augustine said in the passage quoted at the beginning of this reflection, I discern, saying: no, not this, not that either; but yes, this coincides, it fits, it is part of me. In the examination I discover where I have fallen short, failed, lived in the absence of God. I see my sins. Thus, in the examen prayer, I have an opportunity to revisit those painful moments of darkness and rediscover them in the saving love of Christ. The memory of the Lord's Paschal Mystery, of his unbelievable love for me, moves my heart to implore, to repent, to plead for salvation, to call upon the name of the Lord. And thus, whatever I have offered to Christ in humility and penitence as unredeemed I will see redeemed anew. And when a serious matter burdens my adhesion to Christ and what he calls me to be, examination shows me my need for the Church as the place of sacramental forgiveness.

All of this opens up a wider perspective on Baptism. In Baptism, immersed in the life of Christ through the Holy Spirit, we are radically identified with Christ, so that our life is found in his, and Christ already sees us as redeemed. And if the old Adam is still recovering from and caring for the wounds of his corruptible body, it is because the empirical, visible facts do not yet correspond to the true reality. Thus the path has been opened to divinization, an "*ascesis* of love" in which we are divinized to the extent that, immersing ourselves in the memory of Baptism, we increasingly conform to our identity as preserved by God's Wisdom.

We can conclude that in Baptism God gives us his life, eternal life, forming us into his body, the Church. Only by living this reality of redemption can we review the events of the day, our reactions and actions, and carry out discernment in regard to the reality of our life in Christ as his body. Living in familiarity with Christ and the Church, we attain the clear vision of our identity needed to see what is compatible with it and what is not.

PART TWO

The Spiritual Life and
the Examination of Conscience

Now that the foundation and theological principle of the examination of conscience have been reviewed, we come to the concrete aspects of how to understand this spiritual exercise and make it a part of our entire spiritual life.

The Examination of Conscience in Prayer

All that has been said makes it clear that the examination of conscience is chiefly a form of prayer. To examine one's conscience is to listen to one's heart, as described earlier. But we cannot listen to our hearts without being reminded of the Holy Spirit, the Lord who gives life. Our own hearts remind us. In this way we acknowledge the Lord's primacy, recognize him as our life-giving origin, and begin to reason according to the logic of love, of adoration.

The examination of conscience is a prayer. So it is a dialogue, a conversation. . .

The examination of conscience is not carried out only interiorly, where our rationality and self-knowledge alone are at play. The examination of conscience is a purely religious dialogue in which we as believers express our faith and give primacy to our relationship with God. Our silence becomes listening. This listening has a cultural aspect, for its context is the proper position of a human being in the presence of the Lord.

The examination of conscience is a prayer. So it is a dialogue, a conversation in which communication is so real that we begin to look at ourselves with the Lord's eyes. Our spiritual memory of ourselves then grows. With the examination of conscience our spiritual wisdom continually expands. It fills with recollections that are concrete self-images gathered from the memory of God's Wisdom in Christ. And since Christ lives in the Church, the examination of conscience, though very private, always draws from the Church's wisdom and sanctity. In fact, the examination of conscience is made out of love, the holy charity that urges us to become always more ecclesial, always more Trinitarian, so that humanity may become more fully God's image. All Christian *ascesis* finds its meaning in ecclesiality and its foundation in the Trinity. There is no way of growing in holiness if this holiness does not draw the person more deeply into the universal body of the Church, of the Christian community. In this dimension of the Church, of relationships, we find the way of holiness.

Precisely because this conversation with the Lord begins in the heart, which tends to move us toward love, loyalty, coexistence, and the ability to relate, we spontaneously admit our sins, failings, and illusions. Our hearts hold us in relationship, and relationship leads to face-to-face encounters. Only then do we see sin for what it is. This leads to repentance, grief, the request for forgiveness, renewal of commitment, dedication, and covenant.

Confronted with a list of laws and precepts, of models and forms of perfection, one is not stirred to repentance, conversion, or gratitude for God's gratuitous love. Rather, one is moved on a completely different level, which clearly does not belong within the theological framework outlined above. Instead, we carry on a conversation of gratitude and thanksgiving, which often leads us to say beautiful things to our Lord.

So we finish as we began, but with an always more profound recognition of God. We give him the precedence, honor, and glory that are rightfully his.

The Examination of Conscience, Contemplation, and Knowledge

The examination of conscience begins with a prayer to the Holy Spirit and devout silence so that we may enter our hearts and attain a full vision. We ask to be attuned to the voice of our hearts. It is here, at the beginning, that we take on a contemplative attitude. In this sense, we can speak of contemplation on two levels.

The first level is a personal dialogue with the Lord in the Holy Spirit. We contemplate the memory where God unveils his love for us and how he sees us. It is a contemplative attitude in the fullest sense, in which we also listen to the Church's wisdom. We experience communion with the Lord, the holy angels, his messengers, and the saints who have gone before us. In this contemplation we reacquire full spiritual awareness, in which the Spirit imparts to the intellect and emotions a spiritual savor, a delight in love that penetrates the senses in a spiritual way.

The second level of this contemplation is to review all or part of our day. We bring to our immediate memory our encounters and how we related to things, ideas, feelings, and, above all, to the Lord. We look at our lives with the fervor and perspective of the first level of contemplation in which we take on God's view of us. In fact, we must first enter into spiritual contemplation of God's love in order to take on the frame of mind with which to consider the events of the day. Savoring God's love and salvation, we carefully review the day in this light. It is natural to experience traces of the same delight we felt during the day. First we take on the Lord's perspective; then we examine the day from his viewpoint.

This is how the examination proceeds. To first contemplate the day and then look for what was from God is very problematic. That method is full of traps, deceptions, and rationalizations, because it is easy for us to fall into a subtle form of self-admiration, of attachment to our own will and sins. Instead, by starting with how God sees us, with our attention on God's relationship with us, we always begin from an authentically spiritual reality. That reality is completely penetrated by God, by his love, and by his Spirit. By taking hold of our relationship with the triune God, we hold on to the dramatic concrete reality that this relationship has signified, because it involved our creation and redemption. Then we discover the reality that conceals our true image, the vocation to which we are called—admission into the Paschal Mystery, or better, union with Christ in this mystery. Thus, we welcome the gift of paschal wisdom, which contains the memory of God's love. From this perspective we examine ourselves in our daily lives.

As we saw in the first section, those who know the mystery of the cross, of the death and resurrection of Christ, know the mystery of the unity of all things. They know the meaning of history and of all that exists, because the Paschal Mystery is the only true key for interpreting life. For this reason, the contemplative dimension of the examination of conscience is the true door ushering us into genuine self-knowledge and knowledge of others. We understand what is happening to us and what is happening in the world. Thus, an examination of conscience leads us to discover the meaning and sense of our life. For this reason, it begins by listening to God, who speaks to us through people, encounters, events, and history. A good part of the examination of conscience has to do with wisdom; it means knowing how to decipher events and how to understand times, signs, and events. Reviewing our day from the perspective of true contemplation, as we have described, means reviewing it against the background of Christ's Paschal Mystery, in which was wrought our personal salvation and not only salvation in a general sense. Here, according to our affinity with the Paschal Mystery, our spiritual memory recognizes or rejects the realities it revisits.

The contemplative dimension of the examination of conscience is the true door ushering us into genuine self-knowledge and knowledge of others.

Reviving Our Experience

Against this background of the Paschal Mystery, I might discover that some of my actions, attitudes, or thoughts were not lived together with the Lord. They did not have a paschal character. Instead they were lived in distraction, agitation, self-assertion, or egoism. What then must I do?

We have already considered the continuity between human memory and God's eternal memory, between simple recollection and the Lord's efficacious recollection. God makes present the things we recall. We sometimes live or act without conscious reference to the Lord, without having welcomed and remembered his presence, without having given ourselves over to love. Rather, we have remained on our own, using our often unpurified criteria, following vague motivations and letting our self-love get into everything. We know that what we have lived is destined to pass away, to fall into neglect, to disappear. Something may be universally admired, but if it was not done or lived in love, in the presence of the Spirit who gives life, then in the end no trace of it will remain, because only love remains (cf. 1 Cor 13:8). But God looks at everything with love, following every person created in his image with infinite benevolence and in absolute fidelity to his covenant. And in the paschal kenosis, in his Son, God gathers everything and brings it to fruition. In this sense there is a memory of everything we have experienced. In this prayer of examination of conscience, we can ask to enter into this memory to recover our past life. We review it while opening it to the Lord, telling him about all the details and offering it to him. The examination of conscience gives us the opportunity to offer everything that has not been offered before.

We can understand this better if we recall the Gospel episode of the raising of Lazarus. Christ loved Lazarus, so he set out toward Bethany to visit him. But when he arrived, he found that Lazarus was dead, and his sister Martha said to Jesus: "Lord, if you had been here, my brother would not have died. But even now I know that God will give you whatever you ask of him." And Jesus replied: "Your brother will rise again . . . I am the resurrection and the life. Those who believe in me, even though they die, will live, and everyone who lives and believes in me will never die" (Jn 11:21–23, 25–26). This means that Christ's presence is life, that everything experienced in relation to him lives. But if we live as if the Lord were absent, we are given the same opportunity that Lazarus had: a relationship with the Lord that raised him from the dead. Even what has died, as the Lord says, will live if it is with him, if Jesus is welcomed, and if we entrust what has died to him. Thus, in the examination of conscience, when we discover something in our lives that is dead and devoid of love, let us deliberately open it up to the Lord. Let us tell him about it, because, in his Paschal Mystery, he has come to us just as he came to Lazarus in the tomb.

In John 11, Christ calls Lazarus out of the tomb. But the chapter ends with the decision of the high priests and some Pharisees to kill Jesus. In the next chapter Jesus sets off toward Jerusalem, where he will die. Lazarus, then, emerges from the tomb so that Christ may enter it. There is no darkness, no death, no night so dense or sin so terrible that the Lord has not already penetrated. He is waiting for us to return and open these realities to him. And in this openness to him, in this encounter, Jesus communicates to us his perspective on this reality. Our memory is enriched with the recollection of salvation. We have memories of episodes in our lives that, when we discover how Christ remembers them, we see that ours no longer hold true and we need to discard them. His memory does not harden; it transfigures. Love transforms. This leads to genuine religious emotion, without which, in fact, faith becomes sterile, dry, and reduced to mere superficiality. The heart with ecclesial wisdom knows, better than any other judge, which sins require us to kneel in the sacrament of reconciliation.

Only the mercy of God can move us to genuine conversion. Only change made under the impulse and attraction of the love of God endures. We are astounded when, being sinners and guilty of wrongdoing, we discover that God loves us so much that Jesus was crucified for our redemption. The unexpected discovery that we are loved leads to the strongest and most profound motive to renounce evil and embrace a life of virtue. The discovery that we are loved stirs our emo-

The strength of the Lord's love in coming to me will help me to defend myself against sin in the future.

tions and leads us to repent, to recognize and confess sin, and to ask for forgiveness. And the strength of the Lord's love in coming to me will help me to defend myself against sin in the future. The will to improve and to not sin again, the decision to renounce sin, will be effective and sound only if it is founded upon the love that takes me by surprise, and sometimes even brings tears.

Seeing our sins with the Lord's eyes, or actually having the grace to see it *in him* who takes it upon himself, leads to repentance. And repentance makes us hold on more tightly to the Lord and to the Church, the community of believers. Repentance brings us home. On the other hand, to discover our own inadequacy before a law—and not before the face of the Author of the law—weighs us down with a guilt that leads us to isolate ourselves, to flee. This sense of guilt is harmful and corrodes.

The examination of conscience helps us to distinguish between situations that favor our spiritual life and those that hinder its growth and become occasions of sin and temptation. This awareness permits us to avoid these situations and to establish a genuine spiritual strategy.

Discernment

Understood in this way, the examination of conscience consists in the ability to safeguard one's heart and one's eternal salvation. It is especially an exercise of spiritualizing the memory in the climate of wisdom—that is, in the heart—taking into account one's whole person. Thus, it is a process of growing more familiar with the Lord and his Paschal Mystery, of remembering the delight of his love experienced in salvation. It is clear, then, that an examination of conscience in the true, spiritual sense is possible only because of that foundational moment, the event that launches the Christian parable: the experience of forgiveness, of rebirth, of salvation. That is why we always examine ourselves in relation to the experience of salvation. Against this background, the examination of conscience is also a first step toward discernment. In the examen, we take notice of new thoughts that come to us, especially if they return often, and those which are more insistent. We are also attentive to our state of mind, to our clearer, stronger, recurring sentiments, and to persons through whom we have received inspirations. My examination of conscience is the prayerful environment in which I observe and examine all this.

It is helpful to identify certain thoughts, feelings, or inspirations, and to dwell on these for several days, returning to them with each examination of conscience. And since in every examen we strive to see ourselves with the Holy Spirit and the love of God, with the real remembrance of the Paschal Mystery of our salvation, these thoughts may make us feel uneasy. This means that they

The examination of conscience is also a first step toward discernment.

were not spiritual. But it is possible that some thoughts remain—obscure, but increasingly more luminous and familiar. It is then that they should be considered seriously, tested, isolated, and gradually made the object of prayer for discernment, as described in the book *Discernment*.[24] But the groundwork for discernment is laid with an exercise of the memory, as Saint Augustine described in the passage previously quoted. The more we familiarize ourselves with the Lord and his Paschal Mystery, and reinforce the sense of his love, the more our memory is filled with concrete images of how Christ sees us. He suggests to our hearts the things to accept and those to leave aside, ignore, avoid, or watch. For persons who have an orderly spiritual life, the examen offers important starting points for conversation with a spiritual director.

In spiritual direction, people often dwell on their history and stumble along the murky paths of the psyche, seeking explanations for various phenomena, instead of occupying themselves with their ongoing development, which involves the whole person. At first glance, it might seem that the examination of conscience is a prayer in which we focus exclusively on the past. But in examining thoughts, feelings, intentions, inspirations, and intuitions, it really is a prayer by which we guide our personal development. In this sense, the examination of conscience is more akin to preventive medicine than to a medication for an existing condition. On the basis of the examen we gather the subject matter to bring to spiritual direction, where we receive help to carry out discernment and not risk deceiving ourselves.

The examination of conscience, spiritual direction, and confession are closely connected. Unless we are careful and have been trained properly in the sound practice of examining our conscience, our direction sessions can easily deteriorate into purely psychological consultations. We might speak of faith and of religious realities, but solely within the realm of psychology. It is difficult to carry on a conversation about our spirit, our self-understanding with regard to God, our adherence to him. Often even the advice from our director can be reduced to a psychological exercise, sometimes with emphasis on the intellect, sometimes on the will, but involving a sort of "inner hygiene" that cannot be identified with life in the Holy Spirit. This is exactly why many of these conversations take on a therapeutic nature. They can be of great value and importance, but they are not spiritual direction.

If one fails to examine one's conscience or does so poorly, even confession becomes a problem. Either the person does not know what to confess, or does not know why one should confess to a priest. Or, if one's confession is focused too much on self-improvement, he or she might abandon the practice if there is no progress after some time. An examination of conscience intended only to prepare for confession does indeed help us to identify some sins, but it does not lead to an authentic personal relationship with God, our Lord and Savior. It often takes place without real repentance, limited as it is to a mere listing of imperfections. These are confessed to help the person feel better adjusted or more self-satisfied, but without the penitent attitude that leads us to seek forgiveness out of a desire for holiness and to grow in our relationship with God.

The examination of conscience that is open to spiritual direction is a privileged school for reaching the state of prayer that allows for true discernment. Thus, a greater attentiveness to what is new, to a perennial Pentecost, grows within the Church. The examen in its own small way contributes to the great art of discernment. This is certainly the most appropriate context for hearing the voice of the Spirit, who creates today, who suggests new things for today, who is fruitfulness today. "New things" does not mean simply new forms and formulas or new activities. The examen unfolds in an atmosphere of wisdom. Thus, what is "new" especially concerns wisdom, life, and the way we express reality. The "new" consists above all in seeing in a new light not only ourselves but also what happens to us or what is taking place in history. Anything not seen in the proper light can appear false, mistaken, or extraneous. The right light leads us to accept and love realities that we may have contested just a short time before. And the right light is that of the Holy Spirit, who through this exercise instills a welcoming attitude in us.

Growth in Virtue

The examination of conscience leads to continual growth in virtue. As a spiritual exercise connected with wisdom, it helps us proceed in a unified way, without erratic changes and interruptions. By means of the examen, we come to a more precise view of ourselves, communicated to us by God's love through the Holy Spirit in Christ, in whom we have been created and saved. This wisdom is given to us in an increasingly consistent way, so that we truly view ourselves as God does. Throughout the day, this memory prompts the intelligence of the heart to recognize what is spiritual, what truly belongs to us, what improves our lives, what makes us Christ-like. In this way our daily experiences add to our identity, according to a spiritual vision. This leads to growth in wisdom and in love for God and all things. We build up the Christ-like attitudes that are rightly called virtues.

With the examination of conscience the first virtue that grows is the virtue par excellence: charity. In the theological portion of this reflection, we saw how, in its human dimension, charity may not be a completely spiritual reality. It can be mingled with our passions and self-love, and conceal an illusion. The first thing the examination of conscience does is to order our charity according to God's commandments, especially the commandments to love God, and to love our neighbor as ourselves. These commandments have been fulfilled in Christ. Centered on the passion, death, and resurrection of Christ, the examination of conscience brings order to our charity through the art of discernment. In the first place our charity needs to be moderate, which means it should be guided by discernment. Otherwise, even love can become a destructive and ambiguous idol. Although this seems like a paradox, many of the Fathers of the Church warned about the possibility of this grim deception.

Another important virtue that the examination of conscience fosters within us is constancy, perseverance. Without constancy no virtue is really a virtue. And since the examination of conscience is an exercise repeated several times every day, over the years it becomes one of those spiritual practices that form this fundamental attitude of the human heart that is represented by constancy.

There is still another fundamental virtue: humility. The examination of conscience always has some elements of prayer, such as adoration, thanksgiving, petition, and praise. Thus, the examination of conscience confirms and fosters a true attitude of faith that recognizes the Lord as the center of all things, the First, the One from whom everything comes and to whom everything returns. "Souls who thank the Lord work wonders." Those who constantly thank the Lord reinforce their true place before him and before themselves. Every time we give thanks to God, we recognize him as our Lord and Savior, and this fosters in us a similar humble attitude when we approach others.

Awareness of the Divine Life

Because it is an exercise of the spiritual memory, the examination of conscience helps us to become always more aware of our relationship with the Lord and of the fullness of harmony that this produces. The examination of conscience helps us to become aware of how the life and love of God dwell within us.

Thanks to the familiarity with the Lord fostered by this practice, we come to understand how he manifests himself in us and how we live in union with him. This truly helps our faith become more mature. Examination fosters an awareness of our relationship with God and how we respond within that relationship. This awareness of God's gaze upon us is the maturity of faith—that is, it is living in the Lord's presence. Some of the saints used specific techniques to further their awareness of the presence of God, to live with him and in him.

At the same time, the examination of conscience fosters a precise awareness of who we are, how much progress we have made, and how much still lies before us. This awareness of our poverty and misery prevents us from regarding others with arrogance, since we know that whatever we are is by God's grace. Whoever examines him or herself properly is always ready to affirm that everything is a gift of God, that whatever we are is thanks to him, that everything is salvation. We add nothing but our participation, our meager collaboration with the Lord. It is a matter, then, of keeping alive our awareness that we are redeemed persons who no longer have reason to fear, because, despite our poverty and sinfulness, we are so precious in God's eyes that he delivered himself into our hands. The examination of conscience increases this awareness.

Sometimes we can also use the examination to deepen our awareness of certain dimensions of our faith, behavior, and undertakings. We may spend a few weeks prolonging our examination of some particular area of our life where our awareness of being in Christ is not yet rock solid. Often this can help us prepare for confession, because a true awareness of God's love surely comes to us in forgiveness. And we prepare ourselves precisely by contemplating the exorbitant love of God for us, together with the reality that we still hold back and resist his love. Thus, by uncovering our sin or resistance, we stir up the repentance necessary for sacramental reconciliation.

The Particular Examen

If we look into a river, we may see that some rocks in the riverbed are so smooth and clean that the water freely flows over them. But other rocks, covered with moss and mud, block the flow of water. These rocks need to be cleansed, freed from the mud, so that water can flow over them smoothly. The same can be true for us in the examination of conscience. In this process of growing in the awareness of our life-giving relationship with God, we discover areas of greater resistance in us, where the "old man" more easily makes himself felt and asserts himself. Or we become aware that our spiritual memory cannot admit certain attitudes that conflict with our identity as redeemed persons. Yet we are called to accept salvation in these dimensions as well, to entrust them to Christ, to see them in him, to offer them so that they may be transformed into love and freed from self-seeking. Often these vices or habits that remain in us even after we have been forgiven are born and sustained by a mentality of sin that remains active in us. In fact, we are often called to act against this mentality, or our way of thinking.

In this regard, spiritual masters have often suggested the so-called "particular examen." Beginning with a general examen, we gradually isolate an area that has not yet been penetrated by love, that is, by the Holy Spirit. We observe this area for an extended time, examining ourselves on it with greater care and concern. Each day we open this reality to the Lord in such a way that it gradually becomes the main theme of our conversation with God, since we speak to him about it so often. In itself what we are observing is negative, but if we speak to the Lord and offer it to him

The true spiritual struggle . . . is a mystery of love, and a love realized in the way of the Easter Triduum.

often, it becomes a reason to cling tightly to him, to call upon him, to invoke him, to become more deeply aware of our relationship with him. Perhaps, even after a long time, we are still unable to change, but since this dimension is now completely wrapped in prayer, in spiritual humiliations, in invocations, in tears, it becomes a spiritual reality. The action of the Holy Spirit speaks to us of God, orients us toward him, relates us to him, and makes us more like Christ.

Perhaps we will not succeed in changing some of these negative realities even after many years. But if they are the object of this spiritual examen and remain the cause of a closer relationship with God, they lose their venom, like a poisonous serpent that has been rendered harmless. And people notice the difference. The spiritual struggle always benefits everyone. For Christians, perfection does not consist in attaining a sinless state; it consists in the Paschal Mystery, where pain and suffering are consumed by love. When one suffers because of some personality defect or attitude, he or she is concealed in the Paschal Mystery, and God alone knows the impact of this suffering.

It is very difficult to live with our defects, failings, vices, or passions, never managing to free ourselves from them. The true spiritual struggle—which is an art that includes the examination of conscience, especially the particular examen—is a mystery of love, and a love realized in the way of the Easter Triduum. Our duty is to not withdraw but to stand our ground, examine ourselves, ask, implore, try again, begin anew. We will discover the true importance of salvation and the real significance of grace only at the end of life, when the Lord will come to us in a unique and surprising way. And he will come with the very brothers and sisters we wounded with those darker impulses we tried so hard to eliminate, while suffering because those close to us were suffering. The mystery of love, which surrounds every serious ascetic effort, will probably surprise us when we see those same brothers and sisters coming toward us without thinking of the evils they received, because the Lord has transformed those evils for them as well.

PART THREE

Making the Examination

Suggested Method for
the Examination of Conscience

○ I turn my attention to Jesus, my Lord and Savior, to become aware of his presence and my sincere desire to open myself to him. I ask the light of the Holy Spirit. I might help myself to be attentive by reading a text from sacred Scripture, renewing my certainty that the Word of God is permeated by the Holy Spirit. As I recall these words and repeat them, I am encountering the Holy Spirit and opening myself to him. In the same way, it might help me to look at a spiritual image, such as a crucifix, and make the sign of the cross before it. For those who are able, it can be helpful to carry out this exercise in a church or chapel.

○ Focusing on my invocation of the Holy Spirit, with him I enter my heart. In silence, I seek to recollect myself and ask the Holy Spirit to help me to center my thoughts and to think with the intelligence of the heart, that is, with charity. Entering this dimension of the heart means making an act of faith, an act of love toward God. I glorify him and acknowledge him as my Lord and Savior.

○ United with the Holy Spirit in prayer, I draw upon my spiritual memory to see myself as Jesus sees me. He loves me so much that to free me from the power of darkness and death, he offered himself for my sake to insults, violence, and death. He did all this so I could contemplate his face of infinite goodness and indescribable mercy, and see how everything taken up by him and penetrated by his love becomes a beautiful and shining reality. Remembering my redemption in Christ and the manifestation of God's glory in him for my sake, I recognize the overarching meaning of my life. This meaning is concretely present to me as I remember that my salvation has been accomplished in Christ, explained in his Word and in images of him and the saints, and offered to me by the Church. The meaning of my life can, for example, be expressed in my being a disciple of Christ who remains with him at the cross and is the first to reach the empty tomb. Alternatively, I can focus on one of the Lord's sayings, such as, "Whoever wants to serve me, must follow me." In any case, this awareness consists in remaining with the Lord in a personal way.

○ With all of this in mind, I review my day, or part of it, choosing one of various routes. One possibility is how I relate to things, persons, time, God, and myself. Another possibility could involve my encounters with others; or the work I have done; or my most significant, most vehement, most troubling thoughts; or my most intense feelings; or my desires, aspirations, plans. . . . As I look at myself in these difficult situations, observing my thoughts and attitudes in an atmosphere of prayer, I continue to ask the Lord if my spiritual memory corresponds to his—that is, if this is what the Lord sees when he looks at me. As I contemplate the overall meaning of my life and my calling made evident by the redemption, it would be very beneficial to ask the Lord where he is leading me by what I am experiencing, by the attitudes I have taken on during the day, by my actions, encounters, and thoughts. . . . The memory will immediately help me see whether these realities are consistent with my true nature or begin to distort or confuse it, causing tension, disorder, and division. I begin to thank the Lord for everything that in any way reminds me of him and contributes to reinforcing my identity as I have just contemplated in terms of my life's meaning. If I have discovered something that does not correspond to this overall meaning—realities in which I have not lived in relationship with the Lord—I return to them and tell him about them. I speak with him, in detail if necessary, about what happened and how I felt. Meanwhile, like the disciples of Emmaus, I contemplate him in his greatest revelation, that of the paschal Triduum, because in that event he comes closer to every human situation and penetrates all sin and darkness with his love. And with the power of the Holy Spirit, I now see all those realities being renewed, precisely because I am opening them up to the Lord, who revives and transforms them with his presence. I repent, I ask forgiveness, I renew the covenant, and, if necessary, I decide to go to confession.

○ If I become aware of some significant new thought, I recall it and make a special offering of it to the Lord. And for a few days, at this point in the examen, I pause to consider this thought, asking the Lord how he sees it. I always remind myself of my identity, my vocation, and the overall meaning of my life, so that my memory gradually leads me to understand whether that particular thought is to be accepted or not, considered or not.

○ I reflect on what I especially considered in the particular examen. I dwell on it for as long as necessary, looking at the aspect I have chosen to focus on in my spiritual struggle toward maturity. If, for example, I have chosen my tendency to anger, then I review the day with special attention to this aspect. I examine those moments in which my anger erupted, then speak to the Lord in detail about them. I ask the Spirit to impress strongly upon my memory that penetrating gaze of my Lord and Savior, to remind myself of how he sees me in regard to this tendency. If my reflections continue for an extended time, it is helpful to expand my consideration as I talk to the Lord, to see what other aspects of myself are involved in this anger. It can also be helpful to discuss this with my spiritual director, do some spiritual reading, and perform some appropriate penance. For how long? Until I feel that this matter has been permeated with mindfulness of God, and that this tendency is losing the poison of egoism and self-assertion, so harmful to relationships. Here as well, according to the reality I am pondering, I consider the possible need for confession. I conclude with thanksgiving for the Lord's mercy and patience and that of my brothers and sisters. I ask for light, grace, and love.

○ I end by asking the Holy Spirit to support me in this intimacy with the Lord and help me to always see with the eyes of my heart, so I may have a right view of others and the world.

○ As soon as we wake in the morning, we should direct our attention to the Lord, turning to him and invoking the Holy Spirit. Much of the day depends on the first moments after waking. For this reason, we should form the habit of briefly exercising the first points of the examination of conscience: recollection and proper perspective on life.

○ It is also advisable to carry out the examination of conscience at midday and before going to bed. Many spiritual masters placed great emphasis on the conclusion of the day, and the moments before retiring. The last thoughts, sentiments, and images that accompany us before we fall asleep have a certain importance for our spirit during the night. Although in the main examination of conscience we revisit with the Lord the images that were the strongest and the sentiments that were the most forceful and ambiguous, to deprive them of their power, it is not helpful to agitate our conscience in the last moments before we sleep.

○ Moreover, the spiritual masters recommended making the examination of conscience often during the day. Naturally this examination of conscience can be brief. It is not a long prayer, but rather a moment of strong awareness of oneself in God, and of God in one's life.

○ The examination of conscience is not a scrupulous exercise but a joyful experience of redemption. In it we learn a sound realism that strips us of our illusions of moral, disciplinary, or psychological perfection, because we experience the grace of ongoing transformation due to the death and resurrection of Christ. An examination of conscience carried out in this way leads to what was so dear to the heart of Dostoyevsky: feeling free in relation to God, living in freedom as his children. In our times, the question of freedom is still present with all its difficulties. We can nevertheless be sure that if the world sees Christians who are free because they live in love—of which freedom is the essential element—this is the image of real beauty that fascinates and attracts. Only free children can present and bear witness to the true image of the Father.

For Those Who Have Not Had
a Living Experience of God

This morning I stretched out
in a basin of water
and like a relic
I lay in rest. . . .
and here
I came to know better
I am a pliant strand
    of the universe.[25]

Giuseppe Ungaretti

The examination of conscience as has been described here is an exercise of the spiritual memory. It is possible only because there is a memory, an event to be remembered: the salvation in which the Lord has come to us. Without a real experience of salvation, without a personal memory, the examen seems to make no sense. As we know, memory is always concrete, because it is connected to the world of relationships, which is the reality that constitutes the person. And the person is never conceptual, never abstract but always has a face. The memory is connected to that face, which can be pictured, and so it is realistic.

And yet, someone who has not had a concrete experience of salvation, of God's forgiveness and a memory of his face, an experiential awareness of being lifted out of death and darkness, of being washed and cleansed, can still make the examination of conscience. That person can do so in the hope that he or she, too, will experience an encounter with Christ the Lord and Savior. A person who has not yet had a living experience of the Lord cannot make the examination by reviving his or her memory of God. So that person must be careful to avoid the trap of reducing the examination to a sort of checklist, noting the points that apply and ignoring those that do not. That way of making the examen may seem useful, but it conceals a dangerous threat. One finds oneself directing his or her life all alone, and this can reinforce the great illusion that we have the power to reach perfection unaided. To the extent that this happens, it becomes very difficult to avoid self-sufficiency, presumption, and the arrogance that judges others and sees them in a negative way.

But even worse, an exercise like this can reinforce a kind of atheism, a conviction that there is no need to relate to a personal God who can shake up our lives at any moment. Such an examination of conscience can lead to the illusion of being able to manage our own lives and attain salvation by ourselves. And in this case, we can easily content ourselves with an ethical form of religion, in which God is reduced to certain concepts and precepts regarding thoughts, desires, and actions. It is obvious that such a mental construct quickly deteriorates, showing the person's lack of integration. He or she may fulfill the requirements of the most rigorous perfection but fail completely in another respect and justify the inconsistency. Moreover, it is obvious that in our times we face a serious risk of reducing the Church and the Christian faith to a collection of values, especially ethical and moral values.

It is clear, of course, that personal spiritual work is also important. In fact, it is impossible to imagine any kind of growth or progress to maturity without this effort. But we should view this from a completely different perspective than that of faith, in which my commitment, effort, and results are interpreted in light of grace, mercy, and cooperation with the Lord.

There is also another way of conducting the examination of conscience that could be recommended to the unbaptized, as well as to those who have withdrawn from the faith, the life of the Church, and a living relationship with the Lord—or have not yet experienced this.

Within his 1966 film *Andrei Rublev*, the director and writer Andrey Tarkovskiy tells the story of the orphan son of a master bell-maker who succeeds in casting a bell on his own, even though his father never taught him this craft. The boy's father had communicated his passion for his craft, and the son, having seen that the bell is cast by pouring the molten metal into a form dug in the earth, follows a strong intuition that the earth itself can reveal to him the mystery of how to cast the bell. There is a memory, a wisdom that has penetrated all of creation. We only have to listen to it—to establish a real, dialogical relationship with the earth. And the earth will speak to us. Hidden within itself all creation carries the code of the Logos in which and through which all things were created (cf. Col 1:16). This code tells us that creation bears the imprint of the orientation in which it finds its true meaning. It is revealed to those who place themselves before the world in a contemplative attitude. So when we seek to enter into the perspective of charity, we acquire the contemplative attitude that permits us to discover the meaning of things.

There is also a wisdom concentrated in the memory of human beings. This especially comes to us through the Church. I am able to return to the memory that is revealed as my own—vital and efficacious—precisely through the memory of others.

I can be initiated into Wisdom by opening myself to the wisdom of others. "The Holy Spirit is the Church's living memory."[26] The Church's tradition is neither a dead book nor dusty documents in an archive. Rather, the Church is the body of Wisdom that converges in the living Christ.

The charity instilled in us by the Holy Spirit at the moment of our creation sometimes makes itself felt through the fascination and attraction we experience for certain spiritual realities or persons, although they may have lived long ago or far away. By following this attraction, we can begin a genuine dialogue. And by accessing the memory of others we can arrive at the threshold of our own spiritual memory, the threshold of the encounter with the One who formed the spiritual memory of the person I have followed. This kind of ascent to knowledge through the memory and wisdom of others, if carried out correctly, is marked by its gradual and organic growth, by its respectful humility, especially in how we judge others and ourselves, and by its healthy incorporation into concrete daily life. This journey in wisdom also avoids any superficial enthusiasm or rapid progress that congratulates itself on its own achievements.

Freed from an excessively sociological understanding of the Church, we can find an ambient in which every person can draw upon wisdom and the spiritual life. This ecclesial dimension embraces creation, tradition, the magisterium, and the living Christian community. Those who do not have a personal experience of salvation, but who perceive it in the people living around them, can begin to "visit" their world. They can take on the same contemplative attitude with an awareness that leads them to establish relationships with these persons and with the Church. The ecclesial community celebrates the liturgy in which the entire world—the cosmos resurrected together with Christ and subsisting in him—is ordered to the Church. This ambient is already open, and in it each person can begin to follow the threads of a spiritual fabric that has already been woven, in which one will be able to feel oneself an ever more integral part. In this sense, the Church is the true expression of faith in the triune God who is Love, the God who establishes a relationship of love between humanity and himself. The Church is the ambient of faith, discernment, and the freedom of the children of God.

In this light, the seeker can begin to examine his or her life—remaining aware of salvation and of humanity's image in the eyes of the merciful God, because others contemplate it, participate in it, and know it. This person can thus make an examination of conscience by looking at what others have communicated to him or her regarding redeemed humanity. One can examine oneself with a heart open to the mercy of God as the saints have experienced it. One can review one's day and life in openness to the transformative grace of forgiveness as seen and encountered in others. In this way, the seeker begins to act with the heart, with the relational mentality of charity, infusing her or his intelligence with contemplation and love. And considering others, considering their wisdom, this person arrives at a glimpse of a living organism capable of self-revelation, communication, and participation. This organism is itself at the origin of the person's movement and prompts charity in him or her through the power of fascination, attraction, mystery, beauty—all that is connected to life, experience, and Wisdom.

Method for Examining One's Conscience

1. I turn to the Lord, asking the Holy Spirit to place me in his presence. I might foster prayer by looking at a sacred image, by making the sign of the cross. . . .

2. I recollect myself in my heart with an attitude of faith, so as to be able to see myself in my totality before the Lord.

3. I ask for the grace to see myself as God, my Savior, sees me, in light of the overarching meaning of my life. I might repeat some passage from the Word of God that is especially meaningful to me.

4. I review the day, dialoguing with the Lord about everything that has happened at work, in encounters, etc., identifying my most significant thoughts and feelings. I tell him especially whatever in my heart does not correspond to his loving view of me, and I acknowledge when I excluded him and others. I ask his mercy and give thanks.

5. *Particular examination*: I speak with the Lord about the aspects of myself that I am watching with greater spiritual attentiveness at this time. Here, too, I conclude by asking for God's mercy and giving thanks.

6. I ask the Holy Spirit to keep me united to the Lord, that I may continue to see myself and others with the intelligence of the heart.

Notes

1. George Aschenbrenner, "Consciousness Examen," published in *Review for Religious*, no. 31 (1972), pp. 14–21. In it, the author presents the examination of conscience according to the approach of becoming aware of the divine life within us, and as a practical exercise of spiritual life and discernment, above all for religious.

For other writings on this topic, attention should be given to the entry "Examen de conscience" in the *Dictionnaire de Spiritualité* IV (Paris: 1961, 1789–1838), which provides a "history" of the examination of conscience. It identifies similar practices in the ancient world and in non-Christian religions, considering the examen in such cases as synonymous with moments of attention to the interior life and to introspection. The entry then reviews what the appraisal of one's conscience means in the Bible, thus showing that this differs from pagan practices in being not so much a reflection of the soul upon itself, but a process open to a relationship with God, a dialogue in which the believer tests his conformity not to natural reason, by which one discovers the law within oneself, but to God's commandments. In the Fathers of the Church, the historical practice of the examination is united with this relational dimension, developing the ascetic discipline of custody of the heart, attention to thoughts, and the struggle against vice, which in modern terms could be called the "particular examination." In the Middle Ages the examination of conscience was practiced as a spiritual exercise especially within the monastic life, but, as the penitential books demonstrate, it was also linked to sacramental confession, as the penitent's review of his past in order to see where he had failed. It was above all in the fifteenth and sixteenth centuries (*devotio moderna*, Saint Ignatius Loyola) that an organic instruction on the examination of conscience was developed. This was so important for Saint Ignatius that in his Constitutions (no. 261) he proposes it as a daily practice for the Jesuits, in addition to inserting it within the Spiritual Exercises (no. 43). The points that Saint Ignatius proposes are essentially a re-proposal of the ancient *memoria Dei*, a condition for being under the action of grace and cooperating as much as possible with the action of God in us. As a supplement to this entry, see also *"Examen particulier,"* also in the *Dictionnaire de Spiritualité* IV (Paris: 1961, pp. 1838–1849).

For the period following Vatican Council II, in addition to the article by Aschenbrenner, see the entry *"Esame di coscienza"* (by J. Castellano) in the *Dizionario del Concilio Ecumenico Vaticano II* (Rome: 1969, p. 1109), devoted to illustrating what the Council says on this topic, specifically the decree *Presbyterorum Ordinis*, the treatment by A. Cappelletti and M. Caprioli in *Dizionario Enciclopedico di Spiritualità* (ed. E. Ancilli), second edition (Rome: 1990, pp. 903–907), which makes frequent reference to the *Dictionnaire de Spiritualité*; and "Examination of Conscience" (by B. Baynham), in *The New Dictionary of Catholic Spirituality*, ed. M. Downey (Collegeville, MN: 1993, pp. 364–365). [Publisher's Note] Since the original publication of this book in Italian, other works have been published, including *The Examen Prayer* by Timothy Gallagher (The Crossroad Publishing Company, 2006).

2. For anyone who feels the need to delve deeper into the themes that make up the context for the discussion of the examination of conscience, I emphasize that this text is part of a wider perspective. It is part of a series that begins with *Dire l'uomo vol. I: Persona, cultura della pasqua* (2nd ed., Rome: 1997), a vision that attempts to reveal the essential connections between truth, God, the Paschal Mystery of Christ, humankind, sin, and then redemption. It is a vision that also proposes a spiritual form of knowledge. It is connected to *Nel fuoco del roveto ardente* (2nd ed., Rome: 1997), which specifies what the spiritual life is and is not. Moreover, the volume dedicated to discernment titled *Discernment: Acquiring the Heart of God* (Boston: Pauline Books & Media, 2005) is a practical affirmation of a faith in which man and God meet in a free relationship and are able to speak with one another—to communicate and understand each other. I began to develop the theme of memory-knowledge as an essential part of this kind of theological-spiritual vision in *L'arte, memoria della comunione* (Rome: 1994) and in *"La Sofia come memoria creativa da Solov'ëv a Tarkovskij,"* in *Aa.Vv., Dalla Sofia al New Age* (Rome: 1995), I especially explained this in relation to my wall painting of the parousia in the *Redemptoris Mater* chapel. I also tried to express a vision of the action of the Spirit as seen in this chapel as a way that leads to the freedom of creation through the relationship of human beings with God as sons and daughters who participate in the resurrection of Christ (on this, see *"Come mi sono accostato al mosaico della Cappella,"* in M. Apa-O. Clément-C. Valenziano, ed., *La Cappella "Redemptoris Mater" del Papa Giovanni Paolo II* (Vatican City: 1999, pp. 179ff.).

3. Augustine, *Confessions*, X, 18.

4. Maximus the Confessor, *Ambigua*, PG, 91, 113 BC.

5. Vj. I. Ivanov, *Dostoevskij*, Sobr. Soã, IV (Brussels: 1979), 502.

6. Russian Orthodox theologian and philosopher, 1882–1937.

7. John Scotus Eriugena, *De divisione naturae*, 1, 74: PL.

8. S. Frank, *Il pensiero russo da Tolstoj a Losskij* (Milan: 1977), 265.

9. Maximus the Confessor, *Gnostic Centuries* I, 66: PG 90, 1108AB.

10. Athanasius, *Lettere a Serapione*, ep. III, 5–6 (Rome: Città Nuova, 1986).

11. Troparion for Byzantine orthros on Holy Saturday.

12. Gregory of Nyssa, *Against Appolinarius*, 2: PG 45, 1128.

13. Pavel A. Florenskij, *La colonna e il fondamento della verità* (Milan: Rusconi Editore, 1974), 246.

14. J. W. Goethe, *Faust*, I, 1699–1700.

15. T. Spidlik, "Spiritualità slava e religiosità ortodossa," in Aa.Vv., "Lezioni sulla Divinoumanità" (Rome: 1995), 209.

16. Pseudo-Macarius, *Spirito e Fuoco*, Homily 31, 3–4, (Edizioni Qiqajon, 1995), 324–325.

17. Florenskij, *La colonna e il fondamento della verità*, 231.

18. Athanasius, *Orazione II contro gli ariani*, 78: PG 26, 78.

19. William of Saint-Thierry, *Lo specchio della fede*, XX, in SC 301 (Paris: 1982), 137, 139.

20. Florenskij, *La colonna e il fondamento della verità*, 117.

21. Ibid., 405.

22. Y.M. Congar, *La Tradition et les traditions*, II (Paris: 1963), 19.

23. Theophane the Recluse, *Nacertanie christianskago nravoučenija* (Moscow: 1895), 306.

24. Marko Ivan Rupnik, *Discernment: Acquiring the Heart of God* (Boston: Pauline Books & Media, 2005), 86ff.

25. Giuseppe Ungaretti, "*I fiumi*," 1916.

26. *Catechism of the Catholic Church*, 2nd ed. (Washington, DC: Libreria Editrice Vaticana, 1997), no. 1099.

BOOKS & MEDIA

The Daughters of St. Paul operate book and media centers at the following addresses. Visit, call or write the one nearest you today, or find us on the World Wide Web, www.pauline.org

CALIFORNIA
3908 Sepulveda Blvd, Culver City, CA 90230   310-397-8676
935 Brewster Avenue, Redwood City, CA 94063   650-369-4230
5945 Balboa Avenue, San Diego, CA 92111   858-565-9181

FLORIDA
145 S.W. 107th Avenue, Miami, FL 33174   305-559-6715

HAWAII
1143 Bishop Street, Honolulu, HI 96813   808-521-2731
Neighbor Islands call: 866-521-2731

ILLINOIS
172 North Michigan Avenue, Chicago, IL 60601   312-346-4228

LOUISIANA
4403 Veterans Memorial Blvd, Metairie, LA 70006   504-887-7631

MASSACHUSETTS
885 Providence Hwy, Dedham, MA 02026   781-326-5385

MISSOURI
9804 Watson Road, St. Louis, MO 63126   314-965-3512

NEW YORK
64 W. 38th Street, New York, NY 10018   212-754-1110

PENNSYLVANIA
Philadelphia—relocating   215-676-9494

SOUTH CAROLINA
243 King Street, Charleston, SC 29401   843-577-0175

VIRGINIA
1025 King Street, Alexandria, VA 22314   703-549-3806

CANADA
3022 Dufferin Street, Toronto, ON M6B 3T5   416-781-9131

¡También somos su fuente para libros,
videos y música en español!